T0295612

AUDITING

AN OVERVIEW

BUSINESS, TECHNOLOGY AND FINANCE

Additional books and e-books in this series can be found
on Nova's website under the Series tab.

BUSINESS, TECHNOLOGY AND FINANCE

AUDITING

AN OVERVIEW

TIMOTHY CAVENAGH
AND
JACOB RYMILL
EDITORS

nova
science publishers
New York

Library of Congress Cataloging-in-Publication Data

ISBN: 978-1-53615-116-9

Published by Nova Science Publishers, Inc. † New York

CONTENTS

PREFACE

In this compilation, critical aspects of the internal audit function are contrasted in order to provide an insight into the value of internal auditing and, within that, to submit arguments for the implementation and maintenance of an internal audit function.

The authors examine how to optimize the allocation of audit resources over an auditee population with respect to available population statistics. The included survey mainly deals with audit situations where the auditee is assumed to behave rationally and optimize its expected utility based on information regarding the audit strategy.

According to the "International Standards for the Professional Practice of Internal Auditing", internal auditors must always maintain an objective and independent working attitude to perform effectively. However, data indicate that this requirement might often become challenged due to bias-prone situations, eventually leading to false conclusions or even wrong decisions by auditors and management. As such, the authors address selected cognitive biases for internal auditors and potential behavior patterns tempering the effects of these biases.

In common energy audition methods, the efficiency of waste-to-energy power plants is evaluated directly. This method is highly sensitive to the measurement errors of waste mass flow which is difficult determine precisely. Further-more, the direct method does not clarify the sources of energy loss. Using the indirect method which is proposed in this chapter book, the power plant is split into three sub-systems. The overall efficiency is determined by analyzing the multiplication of these sub-systems' efficiency and the internal energy usage.

This final chapter uses case examples to showcase how auditing is a suitable method for clarifying the level of comprehensive, risk-based safety and security management of organizations operating in business and the public sector. The authors encourage organizations to develop their safety and security management system using a risk-based approach.

Chapter 1 - Do internal auditors really add value and improve their organizations' operations as stipulated in the "International Standards for the Professional Practice of Internal Auditing" (IIA, 2018)? Although internal auditors always have to follow their professional standards, this question cannot be simply affirmed. The mandatory value contribution of an internal audit function (IAF) is still disputable among managers and stakeholders. Why? Even if more and more empirical data suggests a positive correlation between internal auditing and improved organizational processes, missing comparable performance metrics for internal auditing are crucial for providing evidence of a value addition. A quantitative, preferably monetary, verification of an added value of assurance and consulting activities of internal auditing is often hard to generate. How can one estimate the financial effect of a correction of an expensive or operatively major project path recommended by internal auditing or how does the corporate reputation and market value of a company increase by a well-designed and effective IAF? But also qualitative aspects such as a 5,000 year-long success story of internal auditing or the positioning as third and last line of defense within the worldwide accepted corporate governance model of the "three lines of defense" were probably no coincidental events. On the other hand, negative aspects such as increasing control costs, a latent antipathy to auditors ("control by colleagues"), the creation of many new internal controls and a too risk-averse operative evaluation might prevent a better acceptance of internal auditing. In the following chapter favorable and critical aspects of the IAF will be contrasted in order to provide an insight into the value of internal auditing and, within that, to submit arguments for the implementation and maintenance of an IAF.

Chapter 2 - According to the "International Standards for the Professional Practice of Internal Auditing" (IIA, 2018) internal auditors always have to maintain an objective and independent working attitude to perform effectively. But theoretical and empirical data indicate that this quality requirement for objectivity and independence might often become challenged due to bias-prone situations and eventually leading to false conclusions or even wrong decisions by auditors and management. Pressure by top management, information asymmetries or limited ressources might cause organizational reasons for auditors' biases, but also internal auditors themselves might create reasons for biases when their career intentions or alibi audits outweigh real findings within audit activities. Interestingly, also psychology might cause many reasons for auditors' biases, e.g., a doubtful self-perception of auditors or cognitive biases like the influence of the physical attractiveness of auditees or repetitive effects of given information. Because cognitive biases have been rarely researched and seldomly communicated, but are especially critical due to their hidden effects, internal auditors should be educated and trained for these situations avoiding wrong or misleading audit findings (α- and β-errors) and thus assuring an effective internal audit function (IAF) as third line of defense within the corporate governance system. Therefore, the main focus in the following chapter lies in selected cognitive biases for internal auditors and potential behavior patterns tempering the effects of these biases.

Chapter 3 - In common energy audition methods, the efficiency of waste-to-energy power plants is evaluated directly. This method is highly sensitive to the measurement errors of waste mass flow which is difficult to be determined precisely. Furthermore, the direct method does not clarify the energy loss sources. Using the indirect method which is proposed in this chapter book, the power plant is split into three sub-systems. These sub-systems are the steam generator, steam cycle and electric generator. The overall efficiency is determined by multiplication of these sub-systems' efficiency and taking into account the internal energy usage. The steam generator efficiency is assessed by the loss method. A thermodynamic model was generated in order to evaluate steam cycle efficiency. Electric generator efficiency is estimated by measuring the output power and energy loss terms. Due to fluctuation in the input waste heating value, steam generator and steam cycle parameters are measured iteratively and an averaged value for efficiency is obtained. The method is applied to a waste-to-energy power plant and the efficiency and energy flow diagram are obtained, consequently. The error analysis shows that the present method is less sensitive to the mass flow rate of the waste as compared to the direct method.

Chapter 4 - This Chapter shows via case examples that auditing is an extremely suitable method for clarifying the level of the comprehensive, risk-based safety and security management (SSM) of organizations operating in business and in public sector. The aim of the Chapter is to encourage organizations to develop their SSM system towards a comprehensive and risk-based approach and to evaluate the level of SSM system through auditing.

In addition, this Chapter introduces three tools developed in Finland that can be applied in SSM audits: 1) The SSM framework drawn up by the Confederation of Finnish Industries in which both safety and security aspects have been included. The framework is widely used both in business and in public sector. 2) National auditing tool 'Katakri 2015' which is designed for assessing organization's ability to protect an authority's classified information and 3) 'Tutor' model designed for inspection or auditing of the SSM developed by the Finnish rescue authority.

This Chapter is based on the study, in which 76 Finnish educational institutions were audited between 2011 and 2014 by using the Tutor model and the SSM framework drawn up by the Confederation of Finnish industries. Moreover, the risk management process in accordance with the standard ISO 31000:2018 has been utilized. Educational institution in the study refers to elementary schools, high schools, vocational schools, universities and universities of applied sciences. The authors experience shows that the safety and security matters are typically discussed and decided in fragmented way or in different contexts without emphasizing the development of comprehensive SSM. Furthermore, the risk management has not been implemented to set strategy, nor to achieve objectives and make decisions in all levels of the organization.

In: Auditing: An Overview   ISBN: 978-1-53615-116-9
Editors: T. Cavenagh and J. Rymill © 2019 Nova Science Publishers, Inc.

Chapter 1

ABOUT THE VALUE OF INTERNAL AUDITING

Hans-Ulrich Westhausen[*]
ANWR GROUP eG,
Mainhausen, Germany

ABSTRACT

Do internal auditors really add value and improve their
organizations' operations as stipulated in the "International Standards for
the Professional Practice of Internal Auditing" (IIA, 2018)? Although
internal auditors always have to follow their professional standards, this
question cannot be simply affirmed. The mandatory value contribution of
an internal audit function (IAF) is still disputable among managers and
stakeholders. Why? Even if more and more empirical data suggests a
positive correlation between internal auditing and improved
organizational processes, missing comparable performance metrics for
internal auditing are crucial for providing evidence of a value addition. A
quantitative, preferably monetary, verification of an added value of
assurance and consulting activities of internal auditing is often hard to
generate. How can one estimate the financial effect of a correction of an
expensive or operatively major project path recommended by internal
auditing or how does the corporate reputation and market value of a

[*] Head of Group Auditing2 Corresponding Author's Email: hans-ulrich.westhausen@t-online.de.

company increase by a well-designed and effective IAF? But also qualitative aspects such as a 5,000 year-long success story of internal auditing or the positioning as third and last line of defense within the worldwide accepted corporate governance model of the "three lines of defense" were probably no coincidental events. On the other hand, negative aspects such as increasing control costs, a latent antipathy to auditors ("control by colleagues"), the creation of many new internal controls and a too risk-averse operative evaluation might prevent a better acceptance of internal auditing. In the following chapter favorable and critical aspects of the IAF will be contrasted in order to provide an insight into the value of internal auditing and, within that, to submit arguments for the implementation and maintenance of an IAF.

Keywords: internal auditing, added value, IIA-standards, effectiveness, three lines of defense, internal audit function, IAF, principal-agent-theory, continuous auditing

1. INTRODUCTION

"Incorporating an Internal Audit function role provides great guidance and assistance to leadership within various firms, companies, etc and in the end, allows for sound financial statement and management oversight of daily business operations. Ideally, establishing such a role, shall result in ensuring that financial statement, company records and company policy and procedures are adhered to in a manner in accordance with the requirements established by the SEC. As guidelines/ requirements are adhered to, citizens of the United States may begin to reestablish their faith in business, with more confidence that company assets/finances are not misappropriated as with World.Com and Enron, a few years prior." (Kim, 2013)

In light of this very affirmative and plausible statement with respect to the implementation of an internal audit function (IAF), it seems rather surprising, when there are oppositional and even completely diametral opinions at the same time (ref. Annex 1). Fundamental critics against the installation of an IAF, especially in small and medium sized companies, are that it limits the operative flexibility due to more and more internal controls, that internal auditing is already maintained in duplicative work by internal SOX- and compliance teams as well as by external auditors and furthermore, an IAF also increases the overhead costs significantly with allegedly no visible value or benefit to the organization.

These extremely critical positions appear rather incomprehensible since internal auditing procedures already go back 5,000 years to the Mesopotamian civilization, and later cultures like the Babylonian, Egyptian, Greek and Roman which also continued with internal controls and dedicated internal auditors (Westhausen, 2016, 63; Sawyer et al., 2005, 3; Brönner, 1992, 664). Since its early beginning, the IAF has been unchallenged over the centuries in ecclesiastical, governmental and in more and more private organizations during soaring international trade activities and the industrialization in the middle of the 19th century. From those years, exactly from 1875, evidence exists about the functioning of a modern IAF in the large German industrial company Friedrich Krupp in Essen (Westhausen, 2016, 65). Internal auditing has been further developing and modernizing until today, e.g., by the foundation of the globally standard setting Institute of Internal Auditors (IIA) in 1941. The Germany chapter, the Deutsches Institut für Interne Revision (DIIR) was founded in 1958. Legal, regulatory and business specific requirements regarding the mandatory or at least strongly recommended implementation of an IAF followed later worldwide, e.g., for public companies, banks, insurances and entities with certain specifics (e.g., organizational size, risk portfolio, public interest). Normative examples are the "Sarbanes-Oxley Act of 2002" with its sections 302 and 404 and corresponding PCAOB-standards that pushed internal auditing forward, and led to the requirement of 2003 that all NYSE-listed companies must have an IAF in place. In Germany, the IAF became mandatory for the first time in 1998, starting with public companies as stipulated in the "Law on Control and Transparency in Business" (KonTraG). But also in Asia the value of the IAF is accepted as

"stock exchanges/governments in China, India, Indonesia, Malaysia, Philippines, Chinese Taiwan, and Thailand require listed companies to have an IA function [IAF]." (Raiborn et al., 2017, 12)

Also the existence of the mankind-long discrepancy between (legal) property and the factual use of property by management (i.e., property right), from which the widely researched principal-agent-conflict as one of the major theoretical foundations of the IAF (ref. Westhausen, 2016, 26; Eulerich et al., 2013, 146) results, hampers the understanding, why such counterpositions against internal auditing and its value are so widespread.

Therefore, the following chapter deals with the gap between the different perspectives on the value of internal auditing. Based on the analysis of the value of internal auditing in theory and literature (section 2), the argumentative approaches for the value addition of internal auditing and the critical ones, challenging the IAF, will be compared with one another (sections 3 and 4). These sections include normative (legal) requirements for an IAF, empirical data about the distribution and the value of internal auditing, but also criticism and reservations against an IAF, mainly based on the examination of the publicised contra comments regarding the proposed and later withdrawn SEC/NASDAQ-rule no. 5645 (2013) about the mandatory incorporation of an IAF in any listed NASDAQ-company by December 31, 2013. Lastly, section 5 concludes this chapter with a discussion of the results.

2. THE VALUE OF INTERNAL AUDITING IN THEORY AND LITERATURE

The value contributing requirement for any IAF in the world can be basically attributed to the "International Standards for the Professional Practice of Internal Auditing" (IIA, 2018). Within these IIA-standards the value adding task of internal auditing is clearly formulated as following:

- The mission of internal auditing is, *"to enhance and protect organizational value by providing risk-based and objective assurance, advice, and insight"* (IIA, 2018, 11).

- The definition of internal auditing describes it as *"an independent, objective assurance and consulting activity designed to add value and improve an organization's operations. It helps an organization accomplish its objectives by bringing a systematic, disciplined approach to evaluate and improve the effectiveness of risk management, control, and governance processes"* (IIA, 2018, 13).
- One main purpose of the IIA-standards is to *"provide a framework for performing and promoting a broad range of value-added internal auditing services"* (IIA, 2018, 18).

Furthermore, also management theory and literature have already been accumulated some research on that issue. The future will probably bring a continuous increase of demand for internal auditing, since an IAF, especially if effective, is probably one of the best governance and project drivers in any organization (remember non-typical audit topics like compliance, data protection, security).

There is only *"one slight problem"* with the value addition of the IAF: the postulated and factually submitted value can often hardly be measured, which is why people easily oversee the value contributing effect of the IAF. This seems to be the *"fundamental evidence problem"* of internal auditing: how to verify or even quantify the positive finalization of a project that was supported by internal auditing in the beginning (i.e., ex ante-consulting) or the corporate reputation and market value of a company increase by a well-designed and effective internal auditing. This is especially due to the fact that internal auditors are often seen as overcritical, risk-averse "paper tigers," hindering the sales team generating new business or stealing the purchase department valuable time, while raising boring compliance questions.

However, in the following subsections 2.1 and 2.2, theoretical and literature implications for the value of internal auditing will be given.

2.1. Theory

Historically, the organizational and management theory about internal auditing has followed the practice with a time lag of a few thousand years. Probably the most prominent theory for the implementation of an IAF, the prical-agent-theory, was developed by Jensen/Meckling in the seventies of the 20th century. But early Mesopotamian records already prooved a long time before Jensen/Meckling that

> "[internal] audits began as far back as 3,500 B.C. The records of a Mesopotamian civilization show tiny marks at the sides of numbers involved in financial transactions. The dots, checks, and tick marks portray a system of verification. One scribe prepared summaries of transactions; another verified those assertions. Internal controls, systems of verification, and the concept of division of duties probably originated at that time." (Sawyer et al., 2005, 3)

Additionally to the historical roots of internal auditing, theoretical concepts are also fundamental to understanding the IAF-role and justifying its organizational value. Therefore, three widely accepted theories about corporate governance issues including internal auditing are summarized in Table 1. Additionally, also the currently remarkable governance model, the "Three Lines of Defense" (TLoD), will be referred to. Although the TLoD is no scientific theory, but a theoretical, generic governance model (such as COSO Internal Control – Integrated Framework, 1992), it implies the fundamental positioning of the IAF as third line of defense within the corporate governance.

According to the TLoD-model any governance system consists of three sequential, combined lines of defense one after another (Westhausen, 2016, 45; IIA, 2013, 2):

- first line of defense: internal, in-process controls (by operative management),

- second line of defense: risk management, compliance, controlling, quality management, inspection etc. and
- third line of defense: IAF.

Table 1. Selected theories and values of internal auditing

No.	Theory	Description of the Theory	Value of Internal Auditing
1)	Principal-agent [Jensen/Meckling, 1976]	Between the principal's side (i.e., shareholder, owner, supervisory board) and the agent's side (e.g., employed CEO, director or manager) exist permanent informational asymmetries and conflicts of interest that can lead to detrimental results for the principal.	One measure to reduce asymmetries, conflicts and mistrust between principal and agent is the implemen-tation of an IAF. Further-more, the IAF can also create confidence among manage-ment and owners (investors) by systematic assurance and consulting activities. An effective IAF might also help the management with the exemption of liability and compensation.
2)	Property rights [Demsetz, 1967]	The enlargement of owner structures in growing organi-zations leads to a thinning of property rights and further-more to a falling involvement (engagement) and control awareness of owners in their property share. The aggrega-tion of this thinning process might cause inefficiencies (e.g., free riding, crowding), negative company performan-ce and even insolvency.	An effective IAF with its transparent, objective audit approach can help organiza-tions to regain trust, motiva-tion and involvement on the owners' side into "their company." This might also transfer positive effects onto the business performance.
3)	Transaction costs [Coase, 1937]	All economic exchanges and business activities are bound to transaction costs (e.g., for information, administration, control). The better a compa-ny manages to optimize/mini-mize the transaction costs, the better the company performs.	For years an IAF has acquired knowledge and experience on how to analyse complex situations or cost structures in order to find the optimal solution with the lowest (transaction) costs and a maximal gain. Therefore, an IAF is a suitable function with specific qualifications to create value by solving transaction cost problems.

Source: Author's own compilation based on Westhausen, 2016, 26 and Eulerich, 2013, 146.

Apart from many other issues influencing the stability of an organization such as the management style or the activity of the supervisory board, the IAF receives the exclusive responsibility as third and last line of defense (*"last man standing"*) to detect potential error or fraud that might have been overseen by the prior two defense lines. Here the enormous relevance and value of the IAF come to light within the TLoD-model, as well as universally in the total corporate governance system.

2.2. Literature

Different perspectives into the research literature suggest a continuously increasing relevance of the value addition of the IAF.

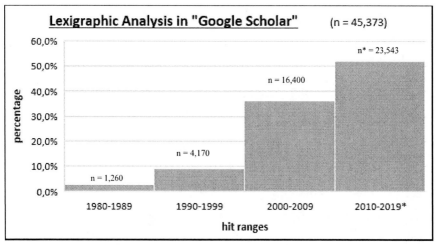

* calculation: 20,600 hits Jan 2010-Sept 2018 (105 months) – 23,543 hits estimated for 2010-2019 (120 months).

Source: author's own compilation.

Figure 1. Histogram of the lexigraphic analysis.

The first perspective is an exploratory literature study (lexigraphic analysis), carried out in the scientific database "Google Scholar" (https://scholar.google.de) Sept 16, 2018. The keyword strings "value"+"internal audit" were entered into "Google Scholar" and listed according to their number of hits (= matches of "value" and "internal audit") within four decades covering almost 40 years of management research, namely 1980-1989, 1990-1999, 2000-2009 and 2010-2019 (latest 15 months were extrapolated).

As presented in the histogram (ref. Figure 1) the growth rate of hits within the last 40 years was tremendous. There were just 1,260 or 2.8% of totally 45,373 hits in the first decade (1980-1989), but 23,543 or 51.9% hits in the last decade (2010-2019). The absolute growth of hits between the first and fourth decade was 22,283 or the 17.7 fold volume of the first decade reflecting an extremely strong increase of relevance of the topic "value of internal auditing" in the management research.

Also the second perspective, a literature review of the last years, reflects a growing research and management interest in the question of the value of internal auditing. Especially in the last five years (2014-2018), research articles have become more in number and material depth. Selected articles, valuable and relevant with respect to the IAF and its organizational worth, are summarized in Table 2. What strikes one immediately is that the evaluations of the IAF tend to get better results the nearer the evaluations are to the time of reporting. Two possible explanatory approaches for that situation are: on the one hand, mostly all evaluations derive from Chief Audit Executives (CAEs), i.e., an one's own picture (self image) of the IAF is reflected here which possibly mirrors the increasing performance pressure on the IAF as a subjective reaction of the CAEs. On the other hand, worldwide management research with the topic "value of the IAF" has also increased continuously, as the lexigraphic analysis (ref. Figure 1) revealed. This might lead to the explanation that the empirical trend of a rising positive IAF-evaluation could also correspond with general positive research results regarding the value creation of the IAF.

Table 2. Literature review of resarch of the IAF value 2014-2018

No.	Article (Authors)	Year	Essential Information
1)	Are Internal Audits Associated with Reductions in Risk? [Carcello et al.]	2018	Empirical study of 69 German operative managers and CAEs states that an IAF • reduces the risk-level of the audited units compared to the non-audited units and • audited units perform better than non-audited units.
2)	Der Mehrwert von Continuous Auditing für die Prüfungs-durchführung, die Berichter-stattung und das Follow-up. Einsatz von Continuous Auditing anhand eines Modellunter-nehmens [Jacka et al.]	2018	Continuous auditing provides a significant added value for operative units as well as for the IAF itself. By establishing and continuously measuring key audit indicators (i.e., risk oriented threshold indicators) auditors and auditees can • earlier than in standard audits (possibly even on a realtime basis), identify process-related weaknesses or target deviations, • initiate ad hoc audits, if threshold values were exceeded and bring the operative unit "back on track" and • realize additional added value, because audit findings will be identified earlier (possibly immediately or even realtime), auditees will start their remediative measures and process improvement earlier, so that the capture of efficiency potentials can start earlier, too.
3)	The Internal Audit Function: A Prerequisite for Good Governance [Raiborn et al.]	2017	The value of the IAF is deduced from several distinctive developments: • many stocks listed young, high-growth technology and Internet-based companies in the US, but also in Europe, Asia and elsewhere, *"have much to gain from an [IAF], even if it is not stock exchange required, because they are more susceptible to internal control weaknesses and fraud than are larger, more established, and financially stronger companies"* (Raiborn et al., 2017, 10), • the NYSE-requirement to have an IAF reflects the persuasion of the NYSE-regulatory body an IAF's benefits outweigh its costs which is similar to value adding, especially to good corporate governance and • an IAF can congtribute value in strategy implementa-tion and quality control.

No.	Article (Authors)	Year	Essential Information
4)	Enquete 2017. Die Interne Revision in Deutschland, Österreich und der Schweiz [Eulerich]	2017	415 CAEs of German, Austrian and Swiss companies express the opinion that the IAF creates added value (4.33) on a Likert-scale from 1 (totally disagree) to 5 (totally agree).
5)	Interne Revision in Verbund-gruppen und Franchise-Systemen. Verbreitung und Qualität der Internen Revision in Unternehmens-netzwerken [Westhausen]	2016	An empirical study of 59 German cooperative and franchise systems resulted in the following: • an IAF can be a crucial stability factor in the network governance (if not in place, the failure risk increases significantly), • the value of an IAF in a network is threefold: preventive (control) effect, reduction of the network risk level and a further additional value as a combination of many singular effects such as process improvements or identification of cashbacks (e.g., in the case of double payments), • value addition effect of a network IAF can be increased by the multiplication of know how, quality best practices and professional support with the legally required responsibility to clarify the potential franchisee by the franchisor about the details of the business precedent to the signature of the franchise contract.
6)	Factors enhancing the internal auditing function's ability to add value to the auditees. Evidences from Italian companies [D'Onza et al.]	2016	Empirical study of 78 Italian CAEs, identifiying three factors that are positively and significantly associated with a value addition of the IAF: • integration of information/feedback from senior management into the setting up of audit plans, • utilization of the IAF as a management training ground and • regular revision of audit methodologies. Furthermore, the study revealed that more than two thirds of CAEs perceive a positive relationship with the auditees and almost 50% of CAEs estimate that their auditees consider internal auditors as peers or partners.
7)	A Study on Internal Auditor Perceptions of the Function Ability to Add Value [D'Onza et al.]	2015	Empirical study of 1,810 CAEs from 107 countries states that • 92% of the respondents believe they add value to their organizations, • the organizational independence of the IAF correlates positively to the capability to create value and

Table 2. (Continued)

No.	Article (Authors)	Year	Essential Information
			• systematic approaches to evaluate internal controls and risks are also positively associated with the value adding ability of the IAF.
8)	Role of internal audit in managerial practice in organisations [Pinto et al.]	2014	Empirical study of 61 listed Brazilean companies (financial managers and directors) states that the management perception of the IAF is that it is a function for • operative support, helping to achieve corporate goals, • continuous assessment as well as mitigation of strategic risks and • -strengthening internal control systems in order to make timely decisions.
9)	Aktuelle Ziele und Zukunfts-perspektiven der Internen Revision [Eulerich]	2014	Based upon 450 opinions of German, Austrian and Swiss CAEs and internal auditors, there exists a common sense that the IAF can generate huge added value for all corporate levels by • maximizing profit, minimizing risks and developing a stable market position (for shareholders/supervisory board/executive management) as well as • optimizing internal processes and functions (for operative management).

Source: Author's own compilation.

Additionally, also several empirical studies of external auditing, consulting and anti-fraud organizations should be mentioned here, although their empirical results were not completely consistent:

- **2018:** 2,690 real cases of occupational fraud from 125 countries with total losses exceeding 7 billion USD total losses, investigated between January 2016 and October 2017, were summarized in the world's largest empirical report about the situation of occupational fraud. Hereafter, the IAF is globally the second most effective anti-fraud detection method with 15%, after whistleblowing/tips with 40% (ACFE, 2018, 17). If an IAF was in place as anti-fraud control, than the average median loss of the reported fraud cases was 46% or 92,000 USD less and the duration 50% or 12 months less (ACFE, 2018, 28).

- **2018:** In the *"2018 State of the Internal Audit Profession Study"* of PwC more than 2,500 board members, senior executives and audit professionals from 92 countries evaluated that up to 75% of the respondents *"view the IA function as providing significant value"* (PwC, 2018, 6). Crucial is how the IAF manages to cope with the challenging technological development (e.g., digitalization, hard- and software, data protection, cybercrime), because a *"lack of technology adoption will result in diminishing value for their organization (56% agree). To play a valuable role in the organization, Internal Audit must enlist innovative tools, skills, and methods for providing assurance"* (PwC, 2018, 5).

- **2016:** Within the KPMG-study *"Mehrwert schaffen durch die Interne Revision" ["Adding Value by Internal Auditing"]* the current and expected IAF-requests of more than 400 CFOs and audit committee members were directly confronted showing negative deviations. The required support during the valuation of risks was delivered by the IAF with 22%, but 57% were expected; a pro-active supply regarding upcoming risks was only delivered with 5% by IAF, but expected with 36% and a sustainable value addition by the IAF was alrady delivered with 33%, but expected at a level of 41% (KPMG, 2016, 3).

- **2015:** The *"2015 State of the Internal Audit Profession Study"* by PwC reflected the opinions of more than 1,300 CAEs, senior management and board members as *"While just 11% [of CAEs] characterize their current internal audit function as providing value-added services and proactive advice for the business, 60% [of CAEs] believe that they will need to be doing this within the next five years. Stakeholders share this same vision ..."* (PwC, 2015, 6).

- **2014:** PwC's *"2014 State of the Internal Audit Profession Study"* of 1,920 CAEs, senior management and board members resulted in *"More than half (55%) of senior management told us that they do* *not believe internal audit adds significant value to their organization. Nearly 30% of board members believe internal audit adds less than significant value. On average, only 49% of senior management and 64% of board members believe internal audit is performing well ..."* (PwC, 2014, 2).

3. ARGUMENTATIVE APPROACH FOR AN IAF

What speaks for the implementation of an IAF? Before one consider the positive sides of an IAF, the first thoughts might be contrary to this: increase of administrative/governance costs, needed office space and technical equipment, sensible worry among the employees, critical questions to management by internal auditors, who – if they are good – are not easy to find in the labor market. So, why that hassle? Can't we operate as in the past without an IAF?

Yes, you can, but empirically the executive and operative (line) management cannot assure the effectiveness of internal controls if a company size exceeds 100 employees (*"control problem of management"*). The critical organizational size is according to management research (ref. Westhausen, 2016, 71; Peemöller et al., 2014, 4) between 100 to 250 employees, when an (institutionalized, departmental) IAF should be implemented, because otherwise the management, irrespective of whether the managers are owners or employed managers, could lose the clear view over more and more complicated operative, adminstrative and financial processes or projects, and also non-standard-threats like manipulation or even fraud. Below 100 employees the control capability of the CEO or CFO or the audit committee might still be sufficient without implementing a formalized IAF, but definitely not if the company operates with less than 100 employees, or in risky markets or with sensitive products or if the corporate structure consists of highly sophisticated, error-prone processes, e.g., thousands or millions of daily transactions.

In the following, a summary of all qualitative and quantitative arguments for an IAF will be displayed in Figure 2, and afterwards five aspects will be explained in more detail.

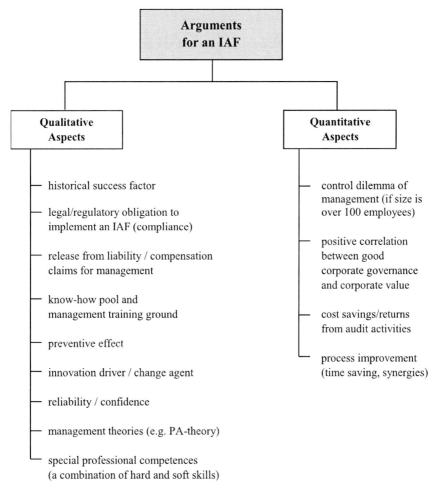

Source: author's own compilation in dependence on Westhausen, 2016, 93.

Figure 2. Arguments for an IAF.

Consequently to Figure 2, selected affirmative aspects for an IAF-implementation could be explained as following:

- **Historical dimension:** As described earlier, the roots of internal auditing go back for more than 5,000 years. All high cultures like the Mesopotamian, Babylonian, Egyptian, Greek and Roman utilized internal auditors in their state and ecclesiastical administrations, e.g., in granaries, in accounting or tax offices. It is said that the *"Greeks were strong believers in control over finances"* and *"ancient Rome employed the 'hearing of accounts',"* an oral verification of records between two officials designed to keep officials in charge of funds from committing fraudulent acts. From this control *("hearing accounts")* the term *"audit"* (from the Latin *"auditus"= "a hearing")* is derived (Sawyer et al., 2005, 4). The success story of internal auditing has continued through industrialization into the digital world of today and will also probably last into the future. How can an "organizational invention," used as a governance and control tool for over 5,000 years, survive several millenia if it doesn't deliver value?

- **Preventive effect:** The preventive effect of internal auditing has already been described in literature – long before theoretical research started – by the Russian author Nikolai Gogol (1809-1852) in his satirical play *"The Government Inspector" or "The Government Auditor"* (1836). Local Russian bureaucrats fixed and adjusted everything and pretended to comply with the rules immediately after the announcement that a government auditor was going to visit the city and to audit its administration. This preventive effect of the IAF exists in any type of organization, irrespective of the company size, legal entity or the organizational structure (e.g., single or group company, network, franchise system). Interestingly, the preventive effect of the IAF unfolds based less upon auditing results (e.g., critical findings) than rather preventively or simply because of the existence of the IAF in the company, i.e., just by its existence and not by its activity (Westhausen, 2016, 90; Amling et al., 2007, 55). Empirically, the continuous auditing activity of the IAF reduces preventively the general error- and spoilage risk in a company (Amling et al., 2007, 52).

- **Dual Compliance:** The incorporation of an effective IAF offers *"dual compliance"*: on the one hand to comply with the requirement to install and maintain an IAF in the organization, either directly by national law (e.g., SOX) or by regulation (e.g., NYSE rules). Consequently, the mandatory requirement to implement an IAF can also arise and disperse with regard to the so called *"transmission effect,"* which means that more and more legal forms of organization are affected by the IAF-implementation requirement (*"The legislator follows the opinion that the IAF-implementation rule for stock listed companies suits other company types, especially limited companies, too. Therefore, it is expected that these other company types also realize this requirement,"* ref. Westhausen, 2016, 42, with regard to the justification for the IAF-implementation by the German legislative). On the other hand, the IAF assures conformance with legal/regulatory requirements within the company, e.g., by regular risk-oriented compliance audits in the operative processes/functions. Thereby the IAF contributes enormous value for corporate management and owner by assuring release from liability and compensation caused by potential non-compliance claims, maintaining a positive reputation of the company and – last but not least – creating a better corporate value. Several empirical studies suggest the correlation of good coporate governance (including an IAF) and better corporate performance (Andres et al., 2013; Jahn et al., 2011; Goncharov et al., 2006).

- **Professional expertise:** An IAF possesses an enormous fund of analytical expertise. This fund covers a methodical clean working approach (e.g., how data and information are to be analysed and interpreted or how to raise the *"right"* questions or how to identify and rate operative risks), an acceptable explanation of auditing results (especially the negative ones) and a good and safe documentation of audit papers. But also the soft skills of internal auditors are rather specific: how to treat auditees in different situations in order to win them as partners, how to convince the management or how to formulate audit findings in a way that auditees agree on the recommended changes. Their knowledge of human nature brings internal auditors in the position to beware of psychological pitfalls like cognitive biases, heuristics and other limitational factors for effective internal auditing. The professional expertise of internal auditors has now been the major reason to utilize that function as a management training ground and a corporate knowledge/know-how pool for decades now (ref. Gutenberg, 1966). Should that not be enough value for an implementation of an IAF, even if voluntary?

- **Innovation driver and change agent:** Internal auditors have a permanent internal (company-wide) informational exchange (e.g., project groups, strategic meetings, discussion with management in the course of internal audits). Additionally, internal auditors also have a wide range of external informational exchanges (e.g., national/international audit colleagues in formal/informal audit circles, seminars, trainings, conferences or just simply contacts on a private, bilateral basis). The almost everyday confrontation with new knowledge or experience, benchmarking and best practices is normal for internal auditors, but not so much for many other employees. The pressure of maintaining their professional qualifications (e.g., CIA, CISA, CFE) requires internal auditors to learn their life long, with 20-40 CPE hours per year. Their assurance and consulting activities require internal auditors to always have a constructive improvement approach in their minds, pushing innovation and change ideas forward. Within the personal profile of internal auditors lies a *"natural potential of an innovator and change agent,"* because of the combination of all these specific characteristics like an analytical strength, communicative power, argumentative skills and a permanent proximity to new concepts and innovative ideas. This *"innovation function"* of the IAF contributes to the the improvement of operative processes and therefore to the value addition of the organization, too (Kundiger, 2007, 222).

Before leaving the perspective supporting an IAF and going on to the section dealing with the negative arguments, the author would like to remind the reader of a rather convincing CEO opinion about the implementation of an IAF:

> "I have always been a firm believer that internal controls are one of the most profitable investments for companies, and that every dollar spent in internal controls would result in a significant return on investment." (Taraboulsi, 2013)

4. CRITICAL ASPECTS AGAINST AN IAF

Depending on the perspective, there supposedly exist different evaluations of the diffusion rate of an IAF in conjunction with the postulated advantage(s) of an IAF, possibly even diametrically opposite. Thus, a relatively small diffusion rate of an IAF can be emanated among small and medium sized companies. Because there are no valid statistical or empirical figures about real implementation and diffusion rates of IAFs, one has to follow estimates by experts. An empirical study of German small and medium sized companies in 2016 resulted in experts' expectations of a diffusion rate of IAFs between 20-50% and an actual diffusion rate in the analysed sample of 31.8% (Westhausen, 2016, 109 and 129). In larger organizations, e.g., listed companies, banks or other financial institutions, an internally installed IAF is anyway legally prescribed and is not questioned. Is therefore an IAF in small and medium sized companies useless and only in place, where legally mandatory, i.e., the IAF is solely legally legitimated for large or financial corporations? The extremely ambivalent IAF-evaluation, depending on the particular observer's perspective, became rather obvious within the discussion of the NASDAQ-rule 5645 in 2013, too: Whereas 96.4% of all NASDAQ-listed respondents were strictly against a mandatory IAF-implementation, exactly 50.0% of the "Non-NASDAQ-respondents" expressed their favor for an undisputed installation of an IAF-function in all NASDAQ-entities, regardless their structural size or other organizational criteria. Hence it can be concluded that the answer about the value of an IAF might turn out totally differently, depending on the party or person being questioned.

However, let's start with an empirical result critically challenging internal auditing:

> "More than half (55%) of senior management told us that they do not believe internal audit adds significant value to their organization. […] On average, only 49% of senior management and 64% of board members believe internal audit is performing well …" (PwC, 2014, 2)

Furthermore, two opinions of experienced managers who expressed their objections against an IAF in 2013 in the course of the NASDAQ-IAF-rule as following:

- *"a mandatory internal audit function would impose significant and unneccesary cost burdens ..."* (Eisenberg, 2013) and
- *"a separate internal control audit function would add significant cost to our Company and would duplicate current company audit activities. [...] My view is that it [an IAF] would only add formality and cost without any additional substance"* (Shallish, 2013).

Even if one knows that the latter critical statements were made by worried CEOs or Executive Directors of smaller NASDAQ-listed companies who should be forced to implement an IAF in 2013 (ref. NASDAQ-rule 5645), beside other comparable types of already existing controls such as frequent SOX-control testing routines, checks and balances, controls by the external auditor and additional controls by the operating management as well as by the audit committee, the statements remain rather offensive and challenging towards anybody on the side of internal auditing.

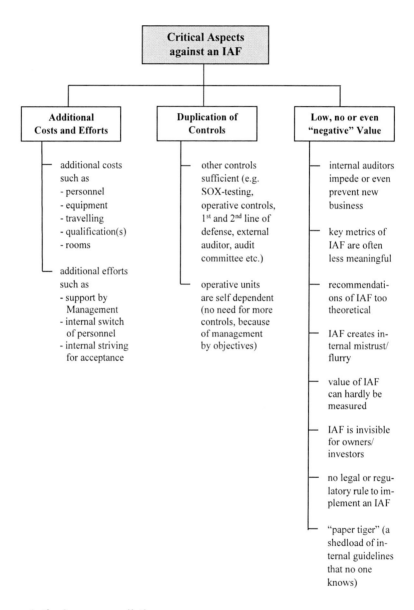

Source: Author's own compilation.

Figure 3. Critical aspects against an IAF.

However, a systematic analysis of critical aspects against an IAF had to be carried out. Before several significant contra arguments are explained, a summary of possible critical aspects against an IAF will be displayed first (ref. Figure 3).

From Figure 3, selected critical aspects against an IAF-implementation could be understood as follows:

- **Duplicative work:** Without any doubt, duplicative work is always tedious. But, controls and audits carried out by the IAF as the third line of defense cannot be duplicative to first and second lines of defense controls. Their control focus is simply another one: since operative controls in the first line are implemented by line management to assure process stability by its process owners themselves (as "in-process-controls"), second line controls are located at a higher entity level and more centered on non-operative, but administrative, governance issues (such as risk aggregations, total quality, legal and compliance issues etc.), as well as "in-process-controls" of functional owners, too. But internal auditing as third line and "last man standing" acts as "ex-process-control," independently from the processual or functional responsibility and therefore not duplicative.
- **Key metrics are often less meaningful:** Within a recent study 1,100 CAEs from 40 countries reported to use KPIs for internal audit activities such as the number of engagements completed (56%), internal audit report issuance timelines (45%) and the number of IAF-observations (21%), according to Deloitte (2018, 19). Other research identified several performance metrics used such as completed versus planned audits, number of recommendations for improvement or training hours per auditor (Bota-Avram et al., 2011, 139). All those KPIs probably have a meaning, but the problem is that those KPIs do not support measuring the quality, effectiveness and value of the IAF. The number of audits or audit reports does not say anything about the quality of the findings. If an audit report needs a couple of days

longer for publication than planned, can have a strong impact on its content. And although auditors have only 10 hours of training per year – albeit very intensive – instead of 20 as planned, it can also have significant positive effects, even if the KPI shows a negative deviation. Therefore, traditional KPIs need to be challenged with more focus on business, risk and "new value added – that is, outcomes that enable Internal Audit to enhance and gauge its impact and influence" (Deloitte, 2018, 19).

- **Value of IAF hardly measurable:** Until today the management research has not yet developed a solid methodology how to quantify the benefit (value) of the IAF as difference between output (expenses) and input (earnings) of internal audit activities. Experts have been trying to indirectly measure the effectiveness by different KPIs, but not directly – and even the latter with limited success only, as research stated: *"Yet the ways of measuring ... internal audit performance are often surprisingly primitive"* (Likierman, 2006, 20). Unfortunately one has to follow Pasternack's evaluation *"the added value of internal auditing as residuum between achievements and costs is in monetary form only exactly quantifiable on the side of the costs, though the achievements of the internal auditing are hardly monetarily measurable"* (Pasternack, 2010, 378).

5. DISCUSSION

During the time of the writing and development of that chapter, the scientific interest and public relevance of the given topic "value of internal auditing" in "Google Scholar" increased by 700 hits of "value"+"internal audit" between mid September and mid October 2018. Within the same period the lexigraphic relevance of "audit committee " increased by about 350 hits and of "internal control" by about 1.200 hits. This finding alone suggests the relevance of the topic internal auditing and its value as well as the engagement on that matter.

Although a proverb says that the management appreciates the presence of an internal auditor, but appreciates it even more if the auditor is about to leave the premises, it does not simply mean that there is no value of the IAF. However, the value of internal auditing is and stays probably a disputed topic, mainly because of its limited quantification. In fact, also other comparable governance or adminstrative corporate functions like controlling, legal or risk management can hardly proove their adding value on a quantified basis. But interestingly, the "value creation question" is mostly raised about the IAF.

Consequently, CAEs have to consider (and even more than in the past), how to improve the marketing of their departments and to demonstrate the corporate benefit of the IAF. In order to become successful with that mission, internal auditing should (ref. Westhausen, 2016, 140, Figure 35)

- increase its value by the multiplication of its audit results (e.g., generic findings, process improvements and control enhancements, which can be promptly rolled out into other corporate organizations without extra efforts and costs – additionally also the initiation of self assessment processes by internal auditing),
- quantify its audit results (even if difficult to measure, but at least as best estimates in terms of saved time, costs or reduced risk levels), including the follow up of the implementation of the recommended/agreed internal measures and
- change the audit perspective from correctness/compliance to efficiency (i.e., more risk-oriented efficiency audits and less, but not no, other audit activities).

Furthermore, CAEs should also pro-actively focus on the known contra arguments against an IAF (ref. Figure 3) such as developing KPIs of internal auditing which are aligned to corporate goals, explain more and better the reasons for particular findings and recommendations (auditees often do not understand the thinking of internal auditors and vice versa) and be always sensitive and aware of duplicative work (e.g., duplication of auditing activities, duplication of controls, duplication of recommended changes). All these activities serve just one idea: The contributed value of the IAF should be made mostly or even completely quantifiable. The methodology of how to quantify the benefit (value) of internal auditing *"would not only be an outstanding scientific merit, but also a step forward towards a crucial improvement of the argumentative basis of the IAF"* (Westhausen, 2016, 180).

But also without that total quantification of the IAF value, experts – even today – argue for the implementation of an IAF due to its obvious value to any organization that implemented it, irrespectively of size, industry or complexity. Even though there are challenging critics against an IAF, they are mostly not against an IAF itself, but against certain issues in the course of internal auditing.

But confidence exists that the value of internal auditing will become clearer and clearer in the future, as expressed by audit experts from the USA and Europe as following:

- *"Establishing a professional internal audit activity should be a governance requirement for all organizations. This is not only important for larger and medium-sized organizations but also may be equally important for smaller entities, as they may face equally complex environments with a less formal, robust organizational structure to ensure the effectiveness of its governance and risk management processes"* (IIA, 2013, 5),
- *"it is probably not exaggerated to state that, even without mandatory legal requirements, an effective IAF must be a component of the Corporate Governance"* (Buderath, 2004, 5) and
- Over 400 CAEs from Germany, Austria and Switzerland strongly agree (an average of 4.33 of 5.00 maximum points at a Likert scale) on the statement that the IAF creates an added value to the organization (Eulerich, 2017, 63, Figure 61).

Last but not least, the creation of an added IAF value should be embedded into efforts towards a positivization of the IAF-perception among management, employees, share- and stakeholders and other related parties. This purposeful reduction of the negative image of internal auditing should essentially include furthering increasingly trustful relationships with line management by *"practice what you preach"* (Rohlf, 2017) and develop the IAF as *"trusted advisor," "change agent"* and *"sparring partner of the executive management"* and an evolving self-conception of internal auditing as *"in the eye of the operative hurricane"* (Eulerich et al., 2018, 92).

REFERENCES

ACFE (2018). Report to the Nations. *2018 Global Study on Occupational Fraud and Abuse.* Accessible at: http://www.acfe.com/report-to-the-nations/2018 [downloaded Sept 26, 2018].

Amling, T., Bantleon, U. (2007). *Handbuch der Internen Revision: Grundlagen, Standards, Berufsstand* [*Manual of Internal Auditing: Fundamentals, standards, profession*]. Berlin, Germany: Erich Schmidt.

Andres, C., Betzer, A., Doumet, M., Limbach, P. (2013). *Auswirkungen guter Corporate Governance und Compliance auf den Unternehmenswert. Kölner Schrift zum Wirtschaftsrecht* [*Impact of good corporate governance and compliance on company value. Cologne font on commercial law*], 1, 92-96.

Bota-Avram, C., Ştefănescu, C. A. (2011). *Methods of measuring the performance of Internal Audit.* Accessible at: https://www.research gate.net/publication/227576321_METHODS_OF_MEASURING_TH E_PERFORMANCE_OF_INTERNAL_AUDIT [downloaded at Oct 3, 2018].

Brönner, H. (1992). Geschichte der Revision [History of the revision]. In: Coenenberg, A. G., von Wysocki, K. (eds.), *Handwörterbuch der Revision* [*Hand dictionary of revision*], 663-670, Stuttgart, Germany: C. E. Poeschel.

Buderath, H. M. (2004): Gastkommentar: Die Interne Revision als Komponente der Unternehmensführung und –überwachung [Guest

Commentary: Internal Audit as a component of corporate governance and oversight]. In: *KPMG's Audit Committee Institute, Bedeutung der Internen Revision in der Corporate Governance* [*KPMG's Audit Committee Institute, Importance of internal audit in corporate governance*], Dec 2004, 4-5.

Carcello, J. V., Eulerich, M., Masli, A., Wood, D. A. (2018). *Are Internal Audits Associated with Reductions in Risk?* Accessible at: https://papers.ssrn.com/sol3/papers.cfm?abstract_id=2970045 [downloaded Sept 21, 2018].

Coase, R. H. (1937). The nature of the firm. *Economica,* 16, 386-404.

COSO (1992). *Internal Control – Integrated Framework.* Jersey City, USA: AICPA.

Deloitte (2018). *Deloitte's 2018 Global Chief Audit Executive research survey.* The innovation imperative. Forging Internal Audits's path to greater impact and influence. Accessible at: file:///G:/NOVA/3.%20 Projekt/manuscript/lu_global-chief-audit-survey-report.pdf [downloaded Oct 3, 2018].

Demsetz, H. (1967). Toward a theory of property rights. *American Economic Review,* 2, 347-359.

D'Onza, G., Sarens, G., Betti, N. (2016). *Factors enhancing the internal auditing function's ability to add value to the auditees.* Evidences from Italian companies (working paper 2016/05). Accessible at: https://cdn.uclouvain.be/public/Exports%20reddot/sshilsm/images/Bett i.pdf [downloaded Sept 5, 2018].

D'Onza, G., Selim, G. M., Melville, R., Allegrini, M. (2015). A Study on Internal Auditor Perceptions of the Function Ability to Add Value. *International Journal of Auditing,* 19, 182-194.

Eisenberg, A. F. (2013). *Comments on NASDAQ Rulemaking. Subject: File No. SR-NASDAQ-2013-03*, From: Alan F. Eisenberg [March 28, 2013]. Accessible at: https://www.sec.gov/comments/sr-nasdaq-2013-032/ nasdaq2013032.shtml [downloaded Sept 15, 2018].

Eulerich, M. (2017). Enquete 2017. *Die Interne Revision in Deutschland, Österreich und der Schweiz (DIIR, IIRÖ, SVIR)* [*Internal Audit in Germany, Austria and Switzerland ([DIIR, IIRÖ, SVIR)*].

Eulerich, M. (2014). Aktuelle Ziele und Zukunftsperspektiven der Internen Revision [Current goals and future prospects of internal audit.]. *Zeitschrift Interne Revision*, 5, 224-230.

Eulerich, M., Wagner, R. (2018). Die Interne Revision in Deutschland, Österreich und der Schweiz (Weitere) Ergebnisse der Enquete 2017 [Internal Audit in Germany, Austria and Switzerland (Further) Results of the 2017 Inquiry]. *Zeitschrift Interne Revision*, 2, 90-93.

Eulerich, M., Velte, P. (2013). Theoretische Fundierung der Internen Revision. Zur ökonomischen Notwendigkeit einer Internen Revision [Theoretical foundation of the internal audit. The economic necessity of an internal audit]. *Zeitschrift Interne Revision*, 3, 146-150.

Goncharov, I., Werner, J. R., Zimmermann, J. (2006). Does compliance with the German Corporate Governance Code have an impact on stock valuation? An empirical analysis. Corporate Governance: *An International Review*, 5, 432-445.

Google Scholar. Permanently accessible at: https://scholar.google.de.

Gutenberg, E. (1966). Der Diplom-Kaufmann als Revisor – Ausbildungsprinzipien der Universität und interne Revision als Praktisches Training für zukünftige Führungskräfte [The Diplom-Kaufmann as auditor - training principles of the university and internal audit as a practical training for future managers]. *Zeitschrift Interne Revision*, 1, 10-24.

IIA (2018). *International Standards for the Professional Practice of Internal Auditing (Standards)* [German edition, version 6.1, Jan 10, 2018]. Frankfurt/M., Germany: DIIR. Accessible at: https://www.diir. de/fileadmin/fachwissen/standards/downloads/IPPF_2017_Standards_ _Version_6.1___20180110.pdf [downloaded Aug 2, 2018].

IIA (2013). *IIA Position Paper: The Three Lines of Defense in effective Risk Management and Control*. Accessible at: https://na.theiia.org/ standards-guidance/Public%20Documents/PP%20 The%20Three%20 Lines%20of%20Defense%20in%20Effective%20Risk%20Managemen t%20and%20Control.pdf [downloaded Sept 21, 2018].

Jacka, C., Persie, K., Schledewitz, H., Wagner, J. M. (2018). Der Mehrwert von Continuous Auditing für die Prüfungsdurchführung, die

Berichterstattung und das Follow-up. Einsatz von Continuous Auditing anhand eines Modellunternehmens [The added value of Continuous Auditing for audit execution, reporting, and follow-up. Use of continuous auditing with a model company]. *Zeitschrift Interne Revision*, 5, 237-243.

Jahn, D. F., Rapp, M. S., Strenger, C., Wolff, M. (2011). Die Wirkungen des Deutschen Corporate Governance Kodex aus Investorenperspektive: Ergebnisse einer Studie [The effects of the German Corporate Governance Code from an investor perspective: results of a study]. *Zeitschrift für Corporate Governance*, 2, 64-68.

Jensen, M. C., Meckling, W. H. (1976). Theory of the firm: Managerial behavior, agency costs and ownership structure. *Journal of Financial Economics,* 4, 305-360.

Kim, A. M. (2013). *Comments on NASDAQ Rulemaking. Subject: File No. SR-NASDAQ-2013-03*, From: Ann Marie Kim [March 12, 2013]. Accessible at: https://www.sec.gov/comments/sr-nasdaq-2013-032/nasdaq2013032.shtml [downloaded Sept 15, 2018].

KPMG (2016). *Mehrwert schaffen durch die Interne Revision [Creating added value through internal audit]*. Accessible at: https://assets.kpmg.com/content/dam/kpmg/pdf/2016/04/kpmg-compliance-internalaudit-mehrwert-sec.pdf [downloaded Sept 26, 2018].

Kundiger, P. (2007). *Die Interne Revision als Change Agent. Veränderungen anstoßen und erfolgreich umsetzen [The internal audit as a change agent. Initiate changes and successfully implement them]*. Berlin, Germany: Erich Schmidt.

Likierman, A. (2006). Measure for measure. *Internal Auditing and Business Risk*, 1, 20-24.

Pasternack, N.-A. (2010). *Qualitätsorientierte Führung in der Internen Revision: Eine theoretische und empirische Untersuchung zu einem Qualitätsmanagement [Quality-oriented leadership in internal audit: A theoretical and empirical study on quality management]*. Hamburg, Germany: Dr. Kovač.

Peemöller, V. H., Kregel, J. (2014). *Grundlagen der Internen Revision: Standards [Fundamentals of Internal Auditing: Standards]*, Aufbau und Führung (eds.). Berlin, Germany: Erich Schmidt.

PwC (2018). 2018 State of the Internal Audit Profession Study. *Moving at the speed of innovation. The foundational tools and talents of technology-enabled Internal Audit.*

PwC (2015). 2015 State of the Internal Audit Profession Study. *Finding True North in a period of rapid transformation.*

PwC (2014). 2014 State of the Internal Audit Profession Study. *Higher Performance by Design: A Blueprint for Change.*

Raiborn, C., Butler, J. B., Martin, K., Pizzini, M. (2017). The Internal Audit Function: A Prerequisite for Good Governance. *The Journal of Corporate Accounting & Finance,* January/February, 10-21.

Rohlf, J. (2017). *5 Ways Internal Audit can add more Value.* https://www.onspring.com/blog/5-ways-internal-audit-can-add-more-value [downloaded Sept 14, 2018].

Sawyer, L. B., Dittenhofer, M. A., Scheiner, J. H. (2005). *Sawyer's internal auditing: The practice of modern internal auditing.* Altamonte Springs, USA: The IIA.

SEC (2013). Release No. 34-69030; File No. SR-NASDAQ-2013-032. *Self-Regulatory Organizations*; The NASDAQ Stock Market LLC; Notice of Filing of Proposed Rule [5645] Change to Require that Listed Companies Have an Internal Audit Function [March 4, 2013].

SEC/NASDAQ (2013). *Comments on NASDAQ Rulemaking.* Notice of Filing of Proposed Rule Change to Require that Listed Companies Have an Internal Audit Function (Release No. 34-69030; File No. SR-NASDAQ-2013-032). Accessible at: https://www.sec.gov/comments/sr-nasdaq-2013-032/nasdaq2013032.shtml [downloaded Sept 17, 2018].

Shallish, R. D., Jr. (2013). *Comments on NASDAQ Rulemaking. Subject: File No. SR-NASDAQ-2013-03,* From: Robert D. Shallish, Jr. [March 28, 2013]. Accessible at: https://www.sec.gov/comments/sr-nasdaq-2013-032/nasdaq2013032.shtml [downloaded Sept 15, 2018].

Taraboulsi, R. R. (2013). *Comments on NASDAQ Rulemaking. Subject: File No. SR-NASDAQ-2013-03*, From: Ramy R. Taraboulsi [April 6, 2013]. Accessible at: https://www.sec.gov/comments/sr-nasdaq-2013-032/nasdaq2013032.shtml [downloaded Sept 15, 2018].

Westhausen, H.-U. (2016). *Interne Revision in Verbundgruppen und Franchise-Systemen. Verbreitung und Qualität der Internen Revision in Unternehmensnetzwerken* [*Internal audit in groups and franchise systems. Dissemination and quality of internal audit in corporate networks*]. Wiesbaden, Germany: Springer Gabler.

APPENDIX

Annex 1: Selected NASDAQ-Comments Regarding Rule No. 5465

Source: SEC/NASDAQ (2013), http://www.sec.gov/comments/sr-nasdaq-2013-032/nasdaq2013032.shtml [downloaded Sept 17, 2018]

From the total of 42 comments, thereof 8 positive (pro IAF-rule of the NASDAQ) and 34 negative (contra IAF-rule), selected extracts from statements are presented in the following.

Pro IAF-Rule

"Internal Audit can not only provide this assurance, it can also be a catalyst for change and improvement within the organization. […] In conclusion, I believe the proposed rule requiring an internal audit function is a good move that would send a very strong and positive message to investors." (Simon J. Parker, Head of Business Assurance, Innospec Inc.)

"I have always been a firm believer that internal controls are one of the most profitable investments for companies, and that every dollar spent in internal controls would result in a significant return on investment." (Ramy R. Taraboulsi, Chairman and CEO, SyncBASE Inc.)

"Incorporating an Internal Audit function role provides great guidance and assistance to leadership within various firms, companies [...] As guidelines/requirements are adhered to, citizens of the United States may begin to reestablish their faith in business, with more confidence that company assets/finances are not misappropriated as with World.Com and Enron, a few years prior." (Ann Marie Kim)

"The IIA believes that a properly structured internal audit function can provide independent, objective assurance and advisory activities that add value and improve organization's operations." (Richard F. Chambers, President and CEO, The Institute of Internal Auditors)

Contra IAF-Rule

"A mandatory internal audit function would impose significant and unneccesary cost burdens ..." (Alan F. Eisenberg, Executive Vice President, Biotechnology Industry Organization)

"A separate internal control audit function would add significant cost to our Company and would duplicate current company audit activities. [...] My view is that it would only add formality and cost without any additional substance." (Robert D. Shallish, Jr., Executive Vice President Finance and CFO, CONMED Corporation)

"We believe this proposed rule change would add another financial burden on us without sufficient evidence that improved controls and/or other added value over the requirements we have today would be the result." (Don Tracy, CFO, MGP Ingredients, Inc.)

"I do not believe it is necessary to require NASDAQ listed companies to have an internal audit function." (Vickie Reed, Sr. Director and Controller, Zogenix, Inc.)

Annex 2: Analysis of NASDAQ-Comments Regarding Rule No. 5465

Sources: SEC/NASDAQ (2013), http://www.sec.gov/comments/sr-nasdaq-2013-032/nasdaq2013032.shtml [downloaded Sept 17, 2018] and author's compilation

Total Comments
   (n = 42)

Comments	n	in %
pro IAF-rule	8	19.0%
contra IAF-rule	34	81.0%
Σ	**42**	**100.0%**

NASDAQ-Listed Companies
   (n = 28)

Comments	n	in %
pro IAF-rule	1	3.6%
contra IAF-rule	27	96.4%
Σ	28	100.0%

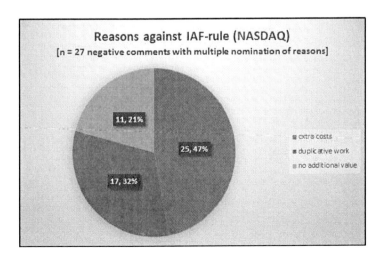

Reasons against IAF-rule (NASDAQ)
[n = 27 negative comments with multiple nomination of reasons]

Other Parties (Non-NASDAQ)
  (n = 14)

Comments	n	in %
pro IAF-rule	7	50.0%
contra IAF-rule	7	50.0%
Σ	14	100.0%

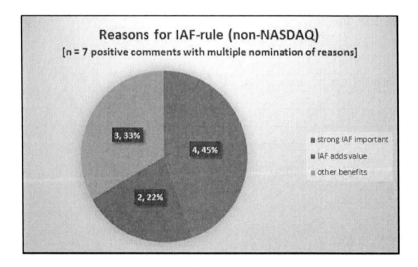

BIOGRAPHICAL SKETCH

Hans-Ulrich Westhausen, PhD

Affiliation: Head of Group Auditing, ANWR GROUP eG

Education: PhD
- 11/2012 - 07/2015: University of Technology, Chemnitz, Germany, doctorate Dr. rer. pol. ("Internal Auditing at cooperatives and franchise systems in Germany")
- 09/1992 - 04/1995: Ruhr-University, Bochum, Germany, M.A. of Sinology, East Asian Economics and General Economics

- 09/1989 - 07/1992: Beijing Language Institute, Beijing, China, B.A. of Modern Chinese
- 11/1987 - 06/1989: University of Leipzig, Germany, basic studies of Journalism and Sinology

Business Address: D-63533 Mainhausen, Germany

Research and Professional Experience:
- PhD (University of Technology, Chemnitz, Germany), research interests include internal auditing (e.g., quality assurance, effectiveness and organizational aspects), fraud prevention and compliance.
- 20 years of experience in internal auditing, holding all major professional certificates such as Certified Financial Services Auditor (CFSA), Certificate in International Accounting (CINA), Certified Information Systems Auditor (CISA), Certified Fraud Examiner (CFE), Certified Control Self-Assessment (CCSA), Certified Internal Auditor (CIA).
- Acting as a seminar instructor for internal auditing and risk management. Latest presentations were about "Interaction of Compliance Management, Internal Audit and Risk Management at the ANWR GROUP" and "Is a process oriented Auditing the better Auditing?."

Professional Appointments:
- since 01/2013: Head of Group Auditing and Compliance, ANWR GROUP eG, Mainhausen, Germany
- 04/2008 - 12/2012: Head of Group Auditing, Risk Management Officer, GARANT Schuh + Mode AG, Dusseldorf, Germany
- 05/2005 - 03/2008: Head of Group Auditing and Group Risk Management Officer, MADAUS Holding GmbH, Cologne, Germany
- 09/2002 - 04/2005: International Auditor, METRO Cash & Carry International GmbH, Dusseldorf, Germany

Publications from the Last 3 Years:

- The "Fraud Report 2018" from the perspective of Internal Auditing – New empirical evidence of the worldwide fraud situation (to be published in *Zeitschrift Interne Revision*, 06/2018).
- Cultural Differences and Similarities between German and Chinese Internal Audit Functions, *Journal of Governance and Regulation, 02/2018*, 57-73, http://doi.org/10.22495/jgr_v7_i2_p6 (co-author Eulerich, M.).
- Internal Auditing, Psychology and Fraud, in: *Advances in Psychology Research*, Band 133, Nova Science Publishers, New York, USA, 2018, 185-209, 978-1-53613-270-0 (Hardcover) und 978-1-53613-271-7 (E-book).
- Requirements to the quality of internal auditing in the change of times – A comparison of quality requirements 50 years ago and today, *Zeitschrift Interne Revision, 01/2018*, 12-17.
- Influencing factors on the payment level of Internal Auditing, *Zeitschrift Interne Revision, 05/2017*, 265-272 (co-author Eulerich, M.).
- The escalating relevance of internal auditing as anti-fraud control, *Journal of Financial Crime, Vol. 24, Issue 2 / 2017*, 322-328.
- The "ACFE-Fraud Report 2016"from the view of Auditing, *Zeitschrift Interne Revision, 04/2016*, 164-169.
- The tech-savvy Auditor, *Internal Auditor, June 2016*, 18-21.
- Challenges at the realization of good Network Governance, *Zeitschrift fur Corporate Governance, 02/2016*, 59-66 (co-author Eulerich, M.).
- Internal Auditing in cooperatives and franchise systems: Empirical results, recommendations and outlook, *Zeitschrift Interne Revision, 02/2016*, 92-99.
- *Internal Auditing at cooperatives and franchise systems* [dissertation], 2016, Springer Gabler, Wiesbaden, Germany, 298 pages, ISBN 978-3-658-12196-9 as print and ISBN 978-3-658-12197-6 as E-book.

In: Auditing: An Overview   ISBN: 978-1-53615-116-9
Editors: T. Cavenagh and J. Rymill © 2019 Nova Science Publishers, Inc.

Chapter 2

COGNITIVE BIASES IN INTERNAL AUDITING

Hans-Ulrich Westhausen[*]
Group Auditing, ANWR GROUP eG,
Mainhausen, Germany

ABSTRACT

According to the "International Standards for the Professional Practice of Internal Auditing" (IIA, 2018) internal auditors always have to maintain an objective and independent working attitude to perform effectively. But theoretical and empirical data indicate that this quality requirement for objectivity and independence might often become challenged due to bias-prone situations and eventually leading to false conclusions or even wrong decisions by auditors and management. Pressure by top management, information asymmetries or limited ressources might cause organizational reasons for auditors' biases, but also internal auditors themselves might create reasons for biases when their career intentions or alibi audits outweigh real findings within audit activities. Interestingly, also psychology might cause many reasons for auditors' biases, e.g., a doubtful self-perception of auditors or cognitive biases like the influence of the physical attractiveness of auditees or repetitive effects of given information. Because cognitive biases have

[*] Head of Group Auditing Corresponding Author's Email: hans-ulrich.westhausen@t-online.de.

been rarely researched and seldomly communicated, but are especially critical due to their hidden effects, internal auditors should be educated and trained for these situations avoiding wrong or misleading audit findings (α- and β-errors) and thus assuring an effective internal audit function (IAF) as third line of defense within the corporate governance system. Therefore, the main focus in the following chapter lies in selected cognitive biases for internal auditors and potential behavior patterns tempering the effects of these biases.

Keywords: internal audit function, IAF, psychology, cognitive bias, overconfidence, IIA-standards, objectivity, independence, debiasing

1. INTRODUCTION

"Perhaps the most commonly cited psychological factor across history, even championed by scholars otherwise promoting alternative theories, is overconfidence." (Coyne et al., 2011, 78)

Our world is full of psychological phenomena and limitations that somehow negatively influence or even manipulate the behavior of people. One significant limitation within human thinking are cognitive biases or "systematic pattern[s] of deviation from norm or rationality in judgment [and decision making], whereby inferences about other people and situations may be drawn in an illogical fashion" (Malizia et al., 2017, 381).

The consequences of cognitive biases reach from incorrect decisions in private lifes (e.g., a purchase of a brand new car that is oversized and too expensive for the young family father) to spurious actions in the business environment (e.g., unjustified sales forecasts of a new product leading to false investments in machinery and personnel). Furthermore, cognitive biases have also led to many unfavorable political results of global dimension. Over centuries until today overconfidence, one of the strongest cognitive biases, has negatively influenced politicans and in conjunction with the "underestimation of the adversary's capabilities" (Levy et al., 1983, 83) even led to awful, unnecessary wars such as the invasion of Napoleon's Grande Armée of Russia (1812), the Soviet intervention in

Afghanistan (1979-1989) or the anti-communist war of the USA in Vietnam (1955-1975). Questionable overconfidence in one's own strength and its potential could also be observed biasing other non-military political decisions such as the slogan of the German Chancellor Mrs. Merkel in 2015 *"Wir schaffen das"* (*"we can do this"*), pretending that the international refugee crisis could be easily handled by the German and European political administrations without naming legal preconditions, budgets or timeframes and also without a democratic consensus among the population. Another "famous" example was the permanent fading out of obvious signals and risks by governmental, regulatory and business organizations turning into the largest financial crisis in the US and global history (2007-2011). The final report of the government commission came to the conclusion, that "despite the expressed view of many on Wall Street and in Washington that the crisis could not have been foreseen or avoided, there were warning signs. The tragedy was that they were ignored or discounted." (National Commission, 2011, xvii)

Not only politicians and military staff are prone to cognitive biases, but also all other walks of professional life like internal or external auditors, scientists, journalists, etc. Exemplary biases, especially influencing general opinion and decision making processes, can be the following:

- one tends to believe the first information given more than later information, regardless the validity of the initial information, and also follows this belief in one's own evaluations and actions (e.g., "if the first number is 120, the sample mean must be somewhere there" or "the first testing result seems plausible, so there is no need for more research"),
- one rationalizes and justifies one's own dissatisfied or even wrong decisions afterwards by adding positive attributes to the object of decision (or negative attributes to the alternative option), often in the course of purchases or investments (e.g., *"oh, the shoes look much better now than in the shop"* or *"though the other hotel was a bit cheaper, it is probably worse than ours, look at its facade"*),

- one expects higher or lower probabilities of the occurrence of an event, depending on the frequency this event happened before, although there is no statistical or empirical evidence for this thinking (e.g., *"after three breakdowns in the last month, it's unlikely that the machine will break down next month again"* or *"after two goals in a row, the player will probably make his hattrick today"*).

The above mentioned cognitive biases, categorized as "anchoring effect", "post-purchase rationalization" (also named "choice-supportive bias")" and "gambler's fallacy" in conjunction with the so called "hot-hand fallacy" are only some examples of a set of 222 researched cognitive biases, 188 (84.7%) thereof listed in the "Cognitive Bias Codex" (The Infomaniac, 2018), here abbreviated as "CBC". But how relevant are cognitive biases for internal auditing and the internal audit function (IAF)? Which are the most common ones? How can they be avoided or at least reduced by internal auditors during their assurance and consulting activities? These questions will be addressed specifically in the following chapter which is divided into eight sections. After the introduction, fundamentals about the impact and relevance of cognitive biases in general and for internal auditing will be presented in sections 2, 3 and 4. Then, in sections 5 and 6, the results of an exploratory literature study about the ranking of cognitive biases for internal auditors, including the top ten biases for internal auditors, are displayed. After that, potential debiasing strategies for internal auditors will be discussed in section 7, before section 8 concludes this chapter with an "Outlook".

2. IMPACT OF COGNITIVE BIASES IN GENERAL

Currently "Google Scholar" (https://scholar.google.de) displays 45,300 scientific links for the keyword string "cognitive bias". From these there are only 15 hits for the year 1970, but 4,730 for 2017 (Aug 26, 2018). If cognitive biases have such an impact on scientific literature, there should also be measurable influence within the political, judicial, social and business world.

The quantification of many biased situations such as the "social expectancy phenomenon" (i.e., reacting as someone believes to be socially correct), systematic answer tendencies (i.e., always answering with "yes", "no" or with "3" on 5-point-Likert scales) or the "Western effect" (i.e., 95% of the world population is not a part of research, but only 5% of "western, educated, industrialized, rich, and democratic societies", Beller, 2016, 107) is a significant bottleneck not only within research in general, but also in specific research with regard to cognitive biases. But even if many biased effects are extremely difficult to verify and measure, more and more empirical studies bring the statistical-mathematical evidence of cognitive biases into light as the following examples show.

The effect of physical attractiveness (*"what is beautiful is good"*, Dion et al., 1972, 285) is one basic effect biasing almost every part of the political and social life. Physical attractiveness has a significant influence on *politics*, e.g., the success in political elections. A study of the election for the German parliament (Bundestag) in 2002 (Klein et al., 2005, 282) revealed that physically attractive candidates had statistically significant better chances to become elected than less attractive persons. Physical attractiveness in total led to a regression coefficient of 0.630 ($p \leq 0.05$), whereas female candidates with a short hair cut even reached a coefficient of 1.332 ($p \leq 0.01$).

Furthermore, physical attractiveness also initiates biasing effects or "extralegal factors" on the *justice system* (*"what is beautiful is innocent"*, Lytle, 2015, 1). A study of 2,235 verdicts came to the result that attractive defendants were punished with significantly lower sanctions (bails/fines) than less attractive defendants (Downs et al., 1991, 544). But many other cognitive factors can also bias the justice system such as the impact of race (i.e., *"jurors are more lenient in their decisions when the juror and the defendant are of the same race"*, Lytle, 2015, 4), prejudices because of sex (i.e., *"female defendants are treated more leniently than male defendants"*, Lytle, 2015, 5) or the defendant's similarity to the juror, e.g., the religious similarity (i.e., "*Jewish defendants were convicted less often than Christian defendants*", Lytle, 2015, 5).

Within the *social environment* the bonus of physical attractiveness is glaring. Attractive individuals (male/female) were seen as significantly (p-value ≤ 0.05) more successful (correlation coefficients 0.90/0.88), more intelligent (0.90/0.88), more appealing (0.90/0.81), more creative (0.84/0.68) and more diligent (0.74/0.78) than less attractive persons (Braun et al., 2003, 44). Beautiful bodies have empirically better professional careers, higher salaries and receive more social respect: 68% of attractive adults had an above-average occupational success comparing to 32% of less attractive adults (Langlois et al., 2000, 402). Candidates holding doctoral degrees will be elected more often into parliament than blue colored workers (Klein et al., 2005, 282). Physically attractive individuals are treated more favorably than physically unattractive individuals ("attractiveness treatment advantage", Binckli, 2014, 40) and attractive children get up to 0.93 better marks at school than their less attractive friends (Dunkake et al., 2012, 152).

Also in the *business world* the effects of cognitive biases are obvious (and costly). Researchers and managers have already identified the impact of cognitive biases and the need to systematically implement debiasing routines within the corporate organizations as the following examples show.

A 2014 survey of 800 board members and chairpersons has ranked "reducing decision biases" as number-one aspiration for improving performance. Another survey of 1,300 executives revealed in 2016, that higher-performing companies use rigorous bias-reducing principles within major decision making processes (Baer et al., 2017, 1). Reducing the effect of bias might lead to up to seven percentage points higher returns (Kahneman et al., 2011, 51). If cognitive biases such as stability biases in capital allocation can be excluded (e.g., dynamic budgeting processes instead of static, generic year after year-estimations), return ratios are between 1.5 and 3.9% higher (Baer et al., 2017, 1). Companies with dynamic capital allocation could grow twice as fast as those which do not change their budgeting principles (Baer et al., 2017, 2). When debiasing high-frequency decisions such as those in credit or insurance underwriting, losses can be reduced by more than 25% (Baer et al., 2017, 2). This can be reached by the implementation of statistical decisions systems based on the analysis of mass data, the use of algorithms and mathematical models instead of manual, personal, intransparent and therefore error- and bias-prone decisions.

As the empirical data from the political, judicial, social and business world suggest, our world is full of cognitive biases that probably influence all spheres of life with a limited possibility of control. Let us now turn from this general perspective to internal auditing.

3. RELEVANCE OF COGNITIVE BIASES FOR INTERNAL AUDITING

The previously mentioned empirical data for the political, judicial, social and business world directly lead to the question, whether cognitive biases could also be relevant for internal auditing by influencing audit results, endangering the independence and objectivity of internal auditors, challenging the effectiveness of internal control systems and eventually the corporate governance at all. The answer to this question is simply "*YES*", although one has to consider that not only cognitive biases might impact the effectiveness of internal auditing, but also other limitational factors such as pressure of management to alter audit findings or the seniority principle ("*the boss is always right*").

When discussing the relevance of cognitive biases for internal auditing, one has to remember the following partials aspects

- mission of internal auditing and requirements regarding an effective IAF,
- limitational factors such as cognitive biases challenging an effective IAF and
- consequences of cognitive biases for internal auditors.

3.1. Internal Auditing: Mission and Requirements

By following its mission (*"to enhance and protect organizational value by providing risk-based and objective assurance, advice, and insight"*, IIA, 2018, 11) the IAF serves as third line of defense in governance structures after internal process controls and risk management (Westhausen, 2018, 188) and therefore as major stability component in many profit and non-profit organizations. While realizing this mission and in order to guarantee qualitative auditing, any IAF around the globe is bound to the "International Standards for the Professional Practice of Internal Auditing" (IIA, 2018). Hereby, the general assumption is, that quality and effectiveness of the IAF can only be considered, if *"taken as a whole, ..., all principles should be present and operating effectively"* (IIA, 2018, 9).

With respect to the "cognitive bias dilemma" the professional standards also focus on the independence and objectivity of the IAF. Following auditing standard no. 1100 (Independence and Objectivity), *"the internal audit activity must be independent, and internal auditors must be objective in performing their work"*. The IIA as the worldwide standard setting body interpretes *independence* as *"the freedom from conditions that threaten the ability of the internal audit activity to carry out internal audit responsibilities in an unbiased manner"* (IIA, 2018, 24). *Objectivity* on the other hand, is *"an unbiased mental attitude that allows internal auditors to perform engagements in such a manner that they believe in their work product and that no quality compromises are made"*(IIA, 2018, 24). Furthermore, individual objectivity has to be ensured, requiring internal auditors to obtain an *"unbiased attitude and avoid any conflict of interest"* (standard no.1120), impairment to independence or objectivity *"must be disclosed to appropriate parties"* (1130) and the quality of communications *"must be accurate, objective, clear, concise, constructive, complete, and timely"*, and also unbiased as one criterion of objective information (2420).

3.2. Limitational Factors in the Auditing Process

But can internal auditors always guarantee the compliance with all professional standards, especially those with correlation to independence, objectivity and an unbiased attitude? Empirical data about internal auditing suggest a slightly different picture:

- A survey of 2,513 worldwide Chief Audit Executives (CAEs) revealed a total conformance rate with all IIA-standards of 54% (Bailey, 2016, 6, exh. 1). Within that, compliance with standard no. 1100 (Independence and Objectivity) came at 82% (Bailey, 2016, 12, exh. 6).
- Another global survey of 10,055 internal auditors led to the insight that 23% of all respondents had already experienced situations where they were directed to suppress or significantly modify valid internal audit findings or reports (Rittenberg, 2016, 23, exh. 13).
- Empirical research identified cultural influence on auditing and standards' conformity with the result, that *"IAFs are not only influenced by the worldwide IIA-Standards, but also by their specific national culture"* (Eulerich et al., 2018, 67).

Consequently, one has to accept that many factors can limit the quality and therefore also the effectiveness of the IAF. Cognitive biases are just one limitational factor among many others like groupthinking (Baer et al., 2017, 3), heuristics (Nisbett et al., 2013, 510) or the seniority principle (Eulerich et al., 2018, 61) that internal auditors have to be aware of when planning and conducting internal audits (see Figure 1).

3.3. Consequences of Cognitive Biases for Internal Auditors

But how strong and relevant is the influence of cognitive biases for internal auditors? From a rather pragmatic point of view one can say: cognitive biases are everywhere, also in the auditing process. The critical and dangerous thing is, that they might induce wrong auditors' evaluations (α- and β-errors[1]) and eventually lead to wrong audit results. Wrong audit results might lead to wrong business decisions like detrimental investments, inefficient process changes or costly lay-offs. To summarize, one can say cognitive biases can have a *strong impact* as well as *high relevance*, not only for any IAF, but also for any company/shareholder/stake-holder.

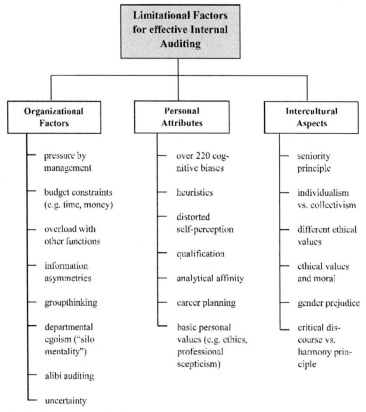

Source: Author's own compilation.

Figure 1. Limitational factors for effective internal auditing.

---

[1] α-error: an orderly situation could be erroneously assessed as defective by the internal auditor with the consequence of unnecessary, costly measures; β-error: a defective situation could also be erroneously assessed as orderly by the internal auditor with the consequence that suitable, mitigating measures to avoid the risk or to assure the achievement of a target will not be initiated.

Apart from possible consequences for companies, share- or stakeholders, wrong audit findings, irrespective of the cause, might also have consequences for internal auditors themselves. Wrong audit findings – depending on the size, recognizability and impact of the error(s) – will always somehow compromise the image of any auditor. The denial of professional qualifications or certifications (e.g., CIA, CFE) and problems on the labor market could be other personal consequences. The employer can fight for civil rights' sanctions such as warning, dismissal or compensation on the internal auditor due to "under performance", unprofessional behavior or a careless working attitude. While fulfilling a "guarantor position" the internal auditor also faces criminal law sanctions such as punitive damage or even prison for intentional or grossly negligent behavior. D&O-insurances might be helpful here, but only partially, because they just cover wrongdoings with minor carelessness, but not intention or gross negligence.

A summary of possible consequences for internal auditors is presented in Figure 2.

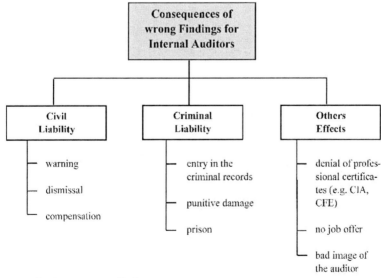

Source: Author's own compilation.

Figure 2. Consequences of wrong findings for internal auditors.

4. COGNITIVE BIASES OF INTERNAL AUDITORS

As said before, cognitive biases as basis for a limited objectivity and independence of internal auditors are everywhere, also in the auditing process. Together with other limitational factors and influences that are extremely difficult to control, they permanently challenge the postulated objectivity and independence in line with an impartial, always sceptical professional attitude of internal auditors. Because of that permanent impact of limitational factors and the impossibility of (absolute) objectivity as required in the professional standards, some researchers even compare that situation with a myth (*"research indicates that impartiality is a myth in audit; [internal] auditors, [...], are influenced by multiple factors as they compile, assess, and report information. Bias, as a counterpoint to objectivity, is prevalent; thus, content is not the only element to be interpreted. Elements that influence their reporting, such as prior expectation and media coverage, may be of equal significance"*, Palmer, 2008, 266).

But which cognitive biases are the most common for internal auditors? With regard to that question, there must be mentioned at first an obvious research and literature gap of bias research of internal auditing, entirely in contrast to the comparable research of external auditing (e.g., Joe et al., 2017; Guiral et al., 2015; Green, 2008).

The published research about the bias situation of internal auditing concentrates less on particular cognitive bias types as in external auditing, but more on *structural bias environments*, which may promote bias situations endangering independence and objectivity for internal auditors (see literature review at Stewart et al., 2010). Those "bias-prone environments" for internal auditors could be:

Assurance versus Consulting

Following the IIA-definition, *"internal auditing is an independent, objective assurance and consulting activity designed to add value and improve an organization's operations*" (IIA, 2018, 13). Although the distribution of both core activities of internal auditing, assurance (auditing) and consulting (advisory), is underresearched (missing empirical data), one can estimate a 80% auditing – 20% consulting ratio, probably with a little tendency towards more assurance activities in the future. According to the "Enquete study" of over 400 IAFs from Germany, Austria and Switzerland the current relevance of consulting activities, e.g., within strategic projects, reached an average index of 2.8 in 2017, whereas auditing activities such as compliance-relevant tasks scored 3.8 (Eulerich, 2017, 61, exh. 59). This trend is also visible with respect to the perspective importance of assurance and consulting activities: the role as strategic consultant will increase by 37.5%, whereas the assurance role, e.g., auditing of cyberrisks, will rise by 87.3% (Eulerich, 2017, 62, exh. 60).

Provided that professional standard no. 1130.A3 ("*The internal audit activity may provide assurance services where it had previously performed consulting services, provided the nature of the consulting did not impair objectivity and provided individual objectivity is managed when assigning resources to the engagement.*") can be assured, then no bias or impairment of internal auditors would be assumed. But one cannot always act on that (theoretical) assumption as there are always limitational factors (ref. sub-section 3.2) and a specific potential bias within the assurance and consulting responsibility of any IAF. This can be exemplarily described as following: Internal auditors have submitted recommendations in the course of a consulting project. Further, the IAF is required to audit the same process/function that was consulted before. A bias tendency arises, because the internal auditors either strongly confirm their prior evaluations/recommendations (irrespective of the quality) or lessen or mask their former consulting recommendations in case they were wrong. Interestingly, according to legal reforms in the European Union ("EU audit reform") coming into effect in 2020, external auditors are obliged to limit their non-audit services (= consulting/advisory) to at most 70% of their audit services ("fee cap"), mainly the check and attestation of annual audit reports or quarterly/semi-annual financial reports. Possible reasoning: reduction of a twofold dependency, from the client's contract volume as well as from the above mentioned responsibility bias within assurance and prior consulting.

Furthermore, a high portion of consulting services by an IAF correlates empirically with a less effective control function of that IAF and is evaluated as less independent (d'Arcy et al., 2012, 127).

Serving Two Masters

In a two-tier governance system the IAF is mostly disciplinarily (i.e., subject to labor law) assigned by either the management/executive board or the supervisory board/audit committee. Empirically, the IAF-subordination in German, Austrian and Swiss companies is at 78.3% with the management board and at 21.7% with supervisory gremiums (Eulerich, 2017, 20, exh. 13). This split of subordination brings the IAF into the "serving two masters-problem", because the existence of different groups of interest might also create high conflict potential (e.g., who approves audit plans/audit reports or who can order the IAF to carry out audits of "the other party", either management board or supervisory gremium or who can authorize "secret audits" without notice to "the other party"). But even if there is no strict separation between operative management and supervisory level as common in one-tier governance systems, there might be similar conflicts in the board of directors about the disciplinary and functional subordination of the IAF, too.

Where does the bias situation come to light here? It can be assumed that the way of communication, the writing style of reports and the set of information submitted, may vary depending on the addressee (e.g., principal, shareholder, managment board, supervisory gremium), although the basic information was all the same which should lead to an unbiased and identical audit report to any of the addressees. But, several experimental studies have indeed detected that a change of reporting lines, e.g., an additional reporting line to the audit committee beside the management, will also change the risk assessment of internal auditors and eventually also the audit result depending on the addressee of the report (d'Arcy et al., 2012, 126).

IAF as Management Training Ground

The use of the IAF as a management training ground is a widespread practice in many companies around the globe. Within that concept, young(er) managers rotate through the internal audit department as part of training them for higher management positions within the organization (i.e., developing interpersonal skills and organizational expertise). Currently, 34% of companies worldwide have formal or informal processes using the IAF as a management training ground, especially in South Asia with an average of 70% (Turner, 2016, 18, exh. 14). The relevant literature about the positive and negative consequences of using that practice has been debated for a long time.

Adverse effects that create unintentional or even intentional bias for the "management trainee auditors" in the internal audit department, are directly caused by the special status of these management trainees: they are in the internal audit department on a limited timescale with no longterm-interest with no incentive to improve the quality of the IAF. They are there mandatorily (otherwise they will not be promoted) and they are dammed not to be too critical towards the auditees (because they might become their later superiors after the traineeship in the IAF). Consequently, the job rotation of biased "management trainee auditors" even "*weakens the effectiveness of their monitoring tasks*" (D'Onza et al., 2016, 5).

Variable Salary (Incentive Compensation) of Internal Auditors

In the opinion of external auditors and also based on experimental studies, variable salaries can negatively influence the power of judgment of internal auditors (d'Arcy et al., 2012, 127).

One can infer that internal auditors might align their audit planning according to those goals defined by the management, e.g., to write 40 audit reports instead of 20 per year or to double the recommendations per audit report compared with today or to increase the efficiency potential in processes (i.e., a switch from qualitative to quantitative auditing). Also the complete audit scope could be changed according to the management goals for variable salary, without any focus on core audit values like risk-orientation, unbiased objectivity and independence.

Cognitive Biases of External Auditors

The working approach of external and internal auditors is rather similar: factual argumentation instead of emotion, evidence of statements, checking instead of believing, transparent audit methodology, objectivity, all based on professional standards. Even if the auditing goals of external and internal auditors are different (i.e., external auditors testify the financial reporting for error-free and credible content, mainly in the name of share- and stakeholders; internal auditors basically assure an orderly, efficient and risk-avoiding existence of processes and functions in the name of internal management and supervision), the presence of bias-prone situations might endanger both types of auditors similarly. Therefore, cognitive biases for external auditors could also be transferred onto internal audit activities.

As a matter of fact, the research of impartiality and limitation of objectivity of external auditors has been significantly more intensive and longer ("*roots back to the mid-1970s*", Kotchetova et al., 2009, 547) than for internal auditing. Also the magnifier of research has been more directed on particular external auditors' biases than in the area of internal auditing. In the following several cognitive biases of external auditors are presented:

- *Confirmation bias:* Both accounting departments and external auditors are interested in longterm relationships which reflect business stability between both sides, career paths for accountants as well as auditors and also trust in given/reported information. But this is just the melting pot for the *"perhaps most commonly known bias seeking information that confirms preexisting beliefs or expectations"* (Wolf, 2018, 2).

- *Overconfidence bias:* External auditors, accountants and probably also other specialists tend to overestimate their ability of being accurate, neutral and bias-immune. But the reality shows that external auditors also overestimate their self-assessment capacities which influences their decisionmaking behavior, i.e., *"how many scenarios are considered, how much information is evaluated, how swiftly decisions are made and how much work is taken on"* (Wolf, 2018, 3).

- *Hindsight bias:* Individuals as well as external auditors, after having been provided with the outcome of an uncertain event, tend to believe that they could have predicted that outcome in foresight. They also deny that their knowledge about the event's outcome had affected their predictions. Experimental studies have proved the manifold existence of the "hindsight bias" for external auditors, in particular while influencing audit judgments, internal control evaluations, audit opinion decisions, preliminary analytical review judgments and going concern judgments (Anderson, 2014, 199).

- *Knowledge bias:* As external auditors often receive information, conclusions or opinions from management about account balances or internal controls, they must decide whether this information is fairly stated. External auditors are then vulnerable to the "knowledge bias" while being unable to ignore previously received information and develop their own assessment independently, e.g., by data analysis, interviews and performing their own walkthroughs of the client's system. The conclusion of one experimental verification of the "knowledge bias" was, *"that [external] auditors exhibit the curse of knowledge bias in that their judgments of the severity of the ICFR problem [internal control over financial reporting] differs based on management's classification of the problem"* (Earley et al., 2008, 1479).

- *Recency bias:* The tendency to put a greater emphasis on the most recent information, is also called the "recency bias", which should be mitigated by professional skepticism within the external auditing process (see statements of PCAOB, IIASB). Experiments with external auditors have revealed that the "recency bias" is always somehow effective with a stronger impact when information is presented sequentially than simultaneously (Koch et al., 2016, 1).

5. Exploratory Literature Study

In the following, the results of an exploratory literature study (lexigraphic analysis) will be presented. The target of that study was to identify the relevance of the 222 cognitive bias categories for the IAF. The research strategy was a lexigraphic analysis of keyword strings of all 222 cognitive biases ("name of bias") in conjunction with "internal audit". Both keyword strings were entered into "Google Scholar" (https://scholar.google.de) and then listed (ranked) according to their number of hits (= matches of "name of bias" and "internal audit").

The lexigraphic analysis was based upon the idea that a higher relevance of bias category should follow a higher number of hits. The analysis was performed Sept 9, 2018 and lasted approximately 3 hours including quality checks and data presentation.

In total, there were 17,793 hits identified for all 222 cognitive bias categories, whereof 188 biases were listed in the "Cognitive Bias Codex" ("CBC"). The hit range was from 0 hits in 86 bias categories up to 3,620 hits in the strongest bias category "persistence" (in the sense of negative insistence or stubbornness). More descriptive statistics of the lexigraphic analysis are summarized in the following Table 1, in Figure 3 and in annex 1 (list of all hits per bias).

The histogram (see Figure 3) demonstrates a relatively strong right skewed distribution, far away from the Gaussian normal distribution. The enormeous predominance of "Zero-hits" of 86 bias categories (or almost

40% of all biases) was not expected. Additionally, the extreme range between "Zero-hits" and 9 bias categories reaching more than 200 hits (4.1%) up to 3,620 hits in the strongest category "persistence", was also unexpected.

Table 1. Descriptive statistics of the lexigraphic analysis

No.	Category	Data	Description
1)	Biases total (n)	222	100.0%
2)	"CBC"-share from 1)	188	84.7%
3)	Hits total	17,793	total number of all hits
4)	Mean	80.1	hit average per 222 biases
5)	strongest bias	3,620 hits	bias category "persistence"
6)	weakest bias	0 hits	86 bias categories had no hit at all

(source: author's own compilation).

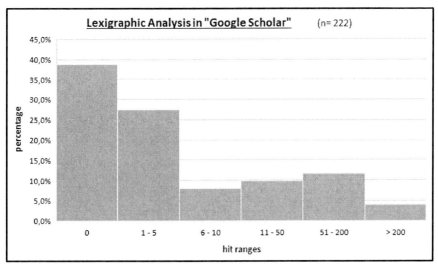

Source: Author's own compilation.

Figure 3. Histogram of the lexigraphic analysis.

6. TOP TEN COGNITIVE BIASES FOR INTERNAL AUDITORS

Following the descriptive statistics, the top ten cognitive biases for internal auditors will now be concentrated on. The ranking of these most relevant biases for internal auditors is the result of the lexigraphic analysis above with the basis assumption of a positive correlation between the number of hits (i.e., "bias"+"internal audit") and the relevance of that bias category.

Table 2 contains the top ten biases for internal auditors with descriptions and "life examples" of how these cognitive biases might influence the working attitude of internal auditors.

Table 2. Top ten cognitive biases for internal auditors

No.	Name of Bias	Description and Examples of the IAF	Number of hits
1	Persistence	Persistence is a personal trait that can be good and bad. If one is persistent, one diligently continues to achieve a goal, even though it is difficult or other people are against it or it is unrealistic. *Ex.: The young internal auditor was very determined to become successful. So, he did all available trainings and certificates he could, but forgot his practical experience and soft skills.*	3,620
2	Prejudice	Prejudice can be an unreasonable, non-rational dislike of particular people or things, or a preference for people or things over other. *Ex.: "You don't need to talk to her, she is 58 and has never used a computer in her life", said the lead internal auditor to the staff auditor, ignoring Mrs. Miller's data analysis ability.*	3,380
3	Physical Attractiveness Stereotype	The physical attractiveness stereotype is the unconscious tendency to treat more attractive people better than less attractive. *Ex.: Nobody thought that she could have stolen the money. She was so pretty and nice, just a darling of everybody ...*	2,590
4	Conservatism	Conservatism is the tendency to retain given procedures like a mantra as well as rejecting one's belief insufficiently (e.g., only partly or not at all) when being confronted with new evidence. *Ex.: "We have never used mass data analytics before. Why should we use that now?", said the CAE to a young IT-auditor.*	2,460

No.	Name of Bias	Description and Examples of the IAF	Number of hits
5	Anchoring	People tend to "anchor" on one trait or piece of information when making decisions (usually the first piece of information acquired on that subject). *Ex.: The manager estimated this year's loss as "probably less than 100 k USD, but not more than 150 k USD". The internal auditors calmed down, until the annual report disclosed a loss of 320 k USD.*	818
6	Overconfidence	One tends to be excessively confident in one's own abilities, capabilities and qualifications. He/she feels "99% certain" in the answer on a certain question. *Ex.: The audit manager was absolutely sure that the audit team could carry out the audit in Russia without any external support (although sufficient language skills were missing).*	556
7	Stereotyping	Stereotyping is the evaluation of a member of a group to have certain characteristics without having any actual information about that individual. *Ex.: Sales managers are always keen on new business despite its risks, whereas internal auditors always prevent new business following their risk-averse working attitude.*	413
8	Gender-Bias	The predisposition to categorize specific characteristics as typical male or female roles/clichés is also called a gender-bias. *Ex.: IT-experts or warehouse managers are usually males, accountants or secretaries are females.*	249
9	Halo Effect	In case of a halo effect, one tends to reason from a person's positive or negative traits to unknown characteristics. *Ex.: The office of that audit manager is always properly tidied up, the desk is clean and all cupboards and shelves are locked. He/she must be successful in his/her job.*	233
10	Social Desirability Bias	Social desirability bias is the tendency to exaggerate socially desirable characteristics in oneself and to understate socially undesirable characteristics. *Ex.: He reported that his audit team had worked 10 hours daily during its last audit engagement. Furthermore, they voluntarily passed the faster but more expensive flight, instead of the time consuming but cheaper train transportation.*	198

Source: Author's own compilation.

As explained before (see sub-section 3.3), the risk of these top ten and all other cognitive biases is that internal auditors could come to erroneous conclusions (α- and β-errors) or wrong recommendations with the consequence of detrimental operative decisions of the management.

As this ranking was derived from a lexigraphic analysis in "Google Scholar", there might be limitations to that exploratory approach, e.g., hits might not be identified due to an inconsistent wording/naming of bias categories throughout the complete literature or not all worldwide research results were officially published and might be not accessible via "Google Scholar". On the other hand, the "Google Scholar"-research should be sufficiently valid to submit generalizable results, i.e., 1,000 hits for bias "A" are obviously more than 100 for bias "B", why bias "A" should be seen as currently more relevant for internal auditors than bias "B". Consequently, the ranking results of the lexigraphic analysis reflect real challenges for any IAF.

Also from the perspective of the author, an internal auditor for almost 20 years now, the top ten biases correlate with his working experience, from which the bias categories persistence, conservatism and overconfidence are noticed particularly often. In order to avoid misunderstanding: persistence in a positive sense as insistency, assertiveness and endurance it is one of the major soft skills an internal auditor should always have (Bünis et al., 2014, 236; Westhausen, 2008, 176), but in a negative connotation as stubbornness it can directly lead to bias in the auditor.

7. DEBIASING STRATEGIES FOR INTERNAL AUDITORS

Even if cognitive biases are unconsciously influencing internal auditors almost everywhere in their evaluations and recommendations with a critical impact on companies and shareholders, one cannot simply accept them. Quite the contrary, one has to ask for potential debiasing strategies in order to sensitize and train internal auditors and eventually reduce the influence level of cognitive biases. Therefore, practitioners and researchers have already been searching for countermeasures against cognitive biases for years.

A summary of possible debiasing strategies is visualized in Figure 4. The summary follows the common separation into five basic strategy categories:

- general strategies,
- specific strategies,
- technological strategies,
- motivational strategies and
- cognitive strategies.

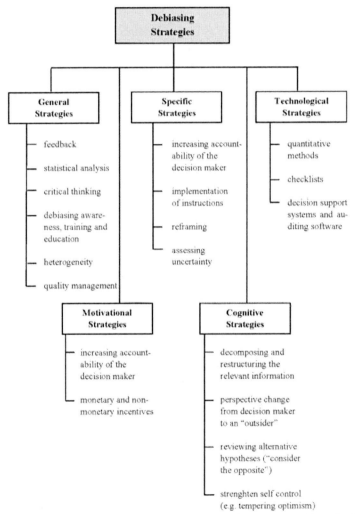

Sources: Author's own compilation based on Aczel et al., 2015, 2; Soll et al., 2014, 12; Larrick, 2009, 316.

Figure 4. Summary of debiasing strategies.

The listed almost 20 independent debiasing strategies cannot always be applied at one time, but partly and gradually. Empirical research has exhibited that continuing debiasing measures eventually lead to less biased internal auditors, e.g., the widely discussed experimental study "*Do fine feathers make a fine bird?*" of Eulerich et al. (2017). The results of that study suggest that anti-bias training and education has had its positive effect: 182 experienced German internal auditors – in comparison to 214 "control subjects" (Bachelor's and Master's degree students from a German university) – decided significantly less biased by the attractiveness of potential fraudsters.

Some other strategic approaches to debiasing evaluation, judgment and desicion making processes are submitted for discussion and/or implementation as following:

Strategy of Modification

Some researchers recommend to debias organizations within a two-stepped strategy of modification of the person and the environment (Soll et al., 2014, 5):

- *1st step:* modifying the decision maker, that "*is to provide people with some combination of training, knowledge, and tools to help overcome their limitations and dispositions*" (Soll et al., 2014, 5). Means can be education (12), cognitive strategies (13) or the use of models to decide (17).
- *2nd step:* modifying the environment, that "*seeks to alter the environment to provide a better match for the thinking that people naturally do when unaided [...], or alternatively, to encourage better thinking*" (Soll et al., 2014, 5). Means can be incentives (19), choice architecture (20) or organizational cognitive repairs (27).

Implemention of a Standardized Evaluation and Judgment Process

Another approach for debiasing is the implementation of a standardized evaluation and judgement process within the organization. This standardized process should consist of the following steps (ref. Glover et al., 2012, 3):

1. define the problem and identify fundamental objectives,
2. consider alternatives (play the "*advocatus diaboli*"),
3. gather and evaluate information,
4. reach a conclusion and
5. articulate and document rationale.

Within that professional evaluation and judgment process the first step is especially crucial, because it is the fundament of the further process, but just step 1 is often skipped by discussion makers. The consequence is as follows: "*Skipping this step [step 1] can result in time wasted solving the wrong problem, and it can severely limit the set of alternatives available for consideration*" (Glover et al., 2012, 3). Although steps 2 - 4 are also essential and important for qualitative judgments and decisions, step 5 should be highlighted here. "*The inability to adequately articulate the rationale for a conclusion often will reveal that a decision may have been based on insufficient information or may not have resulted from a good judgment process*" (Glover et al., 2012, 3). Step 5 creates the basis for liability and compensation claims against management and board.

Do "Bias Audits"

Following the idea of "noise audits" (Kahneman et al., 2016, 41) in order to identify and measure "*irrelevant factors*" within the judgment and decision making process in organizations (e.g., weather, last meal, mood), also "bias audits" could be performed with a similar experimental approach (i.e., setup comparable groups/teams; submit identical problems/cases of daily business that should be solved/decided; measure analyse the differences between the groups and initiate corrective actions. This could be continual monitoring of decisions, eliminating incentives that favor biases, blinding of applications or training employees to detect situations in which biases are likely to occur (ref. Kahneman et al., 2016, 43).

Furthermore, as an experienced internal auditor, the author values the following anti-bias strategies as most useful for an IAF:

- *training and education:* Even if experts are uncertain about the anti-bias strength that education and training have, it is certain is that "*education makes a difference*" (Soll et al., 2014, 12) or "*training seems likely to improve reasoning*" (Nisbett et al., 2013, 527). Then, the question is not whether anti-bias training for internal auditors should be applied or not, but how. More research is needed here to substantiate the value and effect of the different anti-bias strategies.
- *critical thinking:* Critical, independent thinking is one of the core qualifications internal auditors is required to have, especially to maintain an objective and unbiased attitude. Not accidentally, analytical/critical thinking is empirically the number one skill CAEs wish, standing at 64% (Rose, 2016, 3, exh. 2). If internal auditors do not think critically, how can they be the "sparring partner" of the management and board? The complete package of critical thinking entails the ability "*to raise vital questions and problems [...], to gather and assess relevant information [...], to come to well-reasoned conclusions and solutions [...], to think open-mindedly within alternative systems of thought [...] and to communicate effectively with others in figuring out solutions to complex problems*" (Paul et al., 2005, 5).
- *quality management:* Only the maintainance of a quality management system guarantees an effective IAF, including a transparent working approach with an independent and objective fundamental position. This system includes many different control

steps both *during* the operative assurance and consulting processes, and *afterwards* like internal or external quality assessments. The monitoring by key performance indicators as well as the feedback from management or external parties might close the circle of quality. There is no doubt why the auditing standard no. 1300 (Quality Assurance and Improvement Program) requires that "*The chief audit executive must develop and maintain a quality assurance and improvement program that covers all aspects of the internal audit activity.*"

8. OUTLOOK

Our world is full of cognitive biases. Their impact on judgment and decision making can be enormeous, especially when those judgments or decisions were biased and went into costly odysseys of organizations or businesses.

Also internal auditors are not bias-free, as they simply are emotional human beings as everyone else in the world, and do not correspond to the theoretical fiction of a totally rational "*homo oeconomicus*". Due to the significant impact of cognitive biasing in the political, judical, social, business and also auditing world, the question of potential debiasing strategies comes up. Can cognitive biases and other decision making relevant limitational factors such as heuristics or uncertainty (ref. sub-section 3.2) generally become reduced or even deactivated, e.g., by specific training, or do we have to helplessly accept the myth of the ubiquitous curse of cognitive biases? Even if the "*research on debiasing tends to be overshadowed by research demonstrating biases*" (Larrick, 2009, 334), there is still the common sense, that "*the development of new techniques will continue to be the central issue in debiasing research*" (Larrick, 2009, 334).

Supposedly, there will probably always be a gap between pure rational, data based, unemotial (= unbiased) judgments and decision making on the one side and a somehow emotionally influenced (biased) judgment or decision making on the other side. Research suggests that this gap can be continuously reduced by a standardized and therefore almost unbiased decision making process in order to improve the quality of judgments and decision in the future. Especially anti-bias training and education, permanent quality management of all processes in the IAF as well as conformity with the professional IIA-standards can support here. This is also suggested by empirical results and experiments (e.g., Eulerich et al., 2017).

Experts are convinced that *"internal auditors need to have high degrees of emotional and social intelligence"*, reflecting the fact that this psychologically relevant interaction between auditors and auditees *"lies at the core of internal audit assurance activities"* (Dittenhofer et al., 2011, xi). Bearing this in mind, the continuous closing of the gap between internal auditing and psychology (Westhausen, 2018, 185) that has lasted until today should become one of the top priority tasks of internal auditing in the next years.

APPENDIX

Annex 1. List of all cognitive biases (in alphabetical order, n = 222)

No.	Name of Bias	CBC	Hits*
1	absent-mindedness	x	6
2	actor-observer bias	x	3
3	ambiguity bias	x	3
4	anchoring (or focalism)	x	818
5	anecdotal fallacy	x	0
6	anthropomorphism (or personification)	x	8
7	appeal to novelty	x	1
8	appeal to probability fallacy	x	0
9	argument from fallacy	x	0
10	attentional bias	x	1
11	authority bias	x	3
12	automation bias	x	5
No.	Name of Bias	CBC	Hits*
13	availability heuristic	x	82
No.	Name of Bias	CBC	Hits*

14	Baader-Meinhof phenomenon	x	0
15	backfire effect	x	3
16	bandwagon effect	x	74
17	Barnum effect	x	2
18	base rate fallacy (or base rate neglect)	x	6
19	belief bias	x	3
20	Benjamin Franklin effect		0
21	Berkson's paradox		0
22	bias blind spot	x	2
23	bike-shedding effect	x	0
24	bizarreness effect	x	0
25	change bias		0
26	cheerleader effect	x	0
27	childhood amnesia		2
28	choice-supportive bias	x	0
29	clustering illusion	x	0
30	confabulation	x	6
31	confirmation bias	x	188
32	congruence bias	x	1
33	conjunction fallacy	x	4
34	conservatism (or belief revision)	x	2.460
35	consistency bias		6
36	context effect	x	23
37	continued influence effect	x	0
38	contrast effect	x	28
39	correspondence bias (also attribution error)		12
40	courtesy bias		4
41	cross-race effect	x	0
42	cryptomnesia	x	0
43	cue-dependent forgetting	x	1
44	curse of knowledge	x	39
45	declinism	x	1
46	decoy effect	x	0
47	default effect		1
48	defensive attribution	x	1
49	déformation professionnelle		1
50	Delmore effect	x	0
51	denomination effect	x	1
52	disposition effect	x	27
53	distinction bias	x	0
54	Dunning-Kruger effect	x	1
55	duration neglect	x	0
56	effort justification	x	2
57	egocentric bias	x	11
58	emotional reasoning (also emotional argumentation)		7

Annex 1. (Continued)

No.	Name of Bias	CBC	Hits*
59	empathy gap	x	5
60	endowment effect	x	38
61	escalation of commitment	x	151
62	essentialism	x	66
63	exaggerated expectation		3
64	expectation bias	x	8
65	experimenter's bias	x	0
66	extrinsic incentives bias	x	0
67	fading affect bias	x	0
68	false consensus effect	x	7
69	false memory	x	5
70	focusing effect	x	0
71	Forer effect	x	1
72	framing effect	x	59
73	frequency illusion	x	0
74	functional fixedness	x	7
75	fundamental attribution error	x	61
76	gambler's fallacy	x	3
77	gender bias		249
78	generation effect (self-generation effect)	x	3
79	Google effect	x	0
80	group attribution error	x	0
81	halo effect	x	233
82	hard-easy effect	x	1
83	Hawthorne effect		145
84	hindsight bias	x	169
85	hostile attribution bias		0
86	hot-hand fallacy	x	0
87	humor effect	x	0
88	hyperbolic discounting	x	27
89	identifiable victim effect	x	2
90	IKEA bias	x	0
91	illusion of asymmetric insight	x	0
92	illusion of control	x	114
93	illusion of external agency	x	0
94	illusion of transparency	x	7
95	illusion of validity	x	10
96	illusory correlation	x	12
97	illusory superiority	x	2
98	illusory truth effect	x	0
99	impact bias	x	4
100	implicit associations	x	2
101	implicit stereotypes	x	3

No.	Name of Bias	CBC	Hits*
102	information bias	x	61
103	in-group bias	x	27
104	insensitivity to sample size	x	7
105	irrational escalation	x	4
106	just-world hypothesis	x	1
107	lag effect		49
108	Lake Wobegon effect	x	8
109	law of the instrument		0
110	less-is-better effect	x	0
111	leveling and sharpening	x	0
112	levels-of-processing effect	x	0
113	list-length effect	x	0
114	look-elsewhere effect		0
115	loss aversion	x	134
116	magic number 7 + -2	x	1
117	masked man fallacy	x	0
118	memory inhibition	x	0
119	mental accounting	x	108
120	mere exposure effect	x	4
121	misattribution of memory	x	0
122	misinformation effect	x	0
123	modality effect	x	2
124	money illusion	x	11
125	mood-congruent memory bias	x	0
126	moral credential effect	x	0
127	moral luck	x	5
128	Murphy's law	x	69
129	naive cynicism	x	0
130	naive realism	x	21
131	negativity bias (twice in CBC)	xx	7
132	neglect of probability	x	2
133	next-in-line effect	x	0
134	normalcy bias	x	1
135	not invented here	x	89
136	observer effect		34
137	observer-expectancy effect	x	1
138	Occam's razor	x	10
139	omission bias	x	11
140	optimism bias	x	92
141	Ostrich effect	x	1
142	outcome bias	x	36
143	out-group homogeneity bias	x	0
144	overconfidence	x	556
145	pareidolia	x	0
146	part-list cueing effect	x	0

Annex 1. (Continued)

No.	Name of Bias	CBC	Hits*
147	peak-end rule	x	0
148	Peltzman effect	x	1
149	persistence		3.620
150	pessimism bias	x	0
151	attractiveness (also physical attractive-ness stereotype)		2.590
152	picture superiority effect	x	1
153	placebo effect	x	51
154	planning fallacy	x	27
155	positivity effect	x	0
156	post-purchase rationalization	x	0
157	prejudice	x	3.380
158	primacy effect	x	31
159	processing difficulty effect	x	0
160	pro-innovation bias	x	4
161	projection bias	x	3
162	pseudocertainty effect	x	0
163	reactance	x	53
164	reactive devaluation	x	2
165	recall bias		77
166	recency effect	x	67
167	recency illusion	x	0
168	regressive bias		0
169	reminiscence bump		0
170	restraint bias	x	2
171	reverse psychology	x	6
172	rhyme as reason effect	x	0
173	risk compensation	x	104
174	rosy retrospection	x	0
175	scope neglect (also scope insensitivity)		0
176	selective perception	x	99
177	self-consistency bias	x	0
178	self-relevance effect	x	0
179	self-serving bias	x	134
180	Semmelweiß reflex	x	0
181	serial position effect	x	1
182	serial recall effect	x	0
183	sexual overperception bias/sexual underperception bias		0
184	shared information bias		1
185	sociability bias of language		0
186	social comparison bias	x	0
187	social desirability bias	x	198
188	source confusion	x	1
189	spacing effect	x	2

No.	Name of Bias	CBC	Hits[*]
190	spotlight effect	x	2
191	status quo bias	x	70
192	stereotypical bias	x	0
193	stereotyping	x	413
No.	Name of Bias	CBC	Hits[*]
194	subadditivity effect	x	3
195	subjective validation	x	3
196	suffix effect	x	0
197	suggestibility	x	26
198	sunk cost fallacy	x	7
199	surrogation		25
200	survivorship bias	x	104
201	system justification	x	28
202	telescoping effect	x	0
203	testing effect	x	8
204	third-person effect	x	5
205	time-saving bias	x	0
206	tip of the tongue effect	x	0
207	trait ascription bias	x	0
208	travis syndrome		0
209	triviality (also Parkinson's law of triviality)	x	41
210	turkey illusion		1
211	ultimate attribution error	x	4
212	unit bias	x	0
213	verbatim effect		0
214	von Restorff effect	x	0
215	Weber-Fechner law	x	2
216	well-traveled road effect	x	0
217	"women are wonderful" effect		0
218	worse-than-average effect		0
219	Zeigarnik effect		0
220	zero-risk bias	x	0
221	zero-sum bias	x	0
222	two-factor theory of emotion		0
Σ		**188**	**17.793**

Sources: Cognitive Bias Codex/"CBC" (The Infomaniac, 2018) and author's compilation of other research sources.

[*] Hits: number of results (matches) at the keyword search of ["name of bias"+"internal audit"], Google Scholar (https://scholar.google.de), analysed Sept 9, 2018.

REFERENCES

Aczel, B., Bago, B., Szollosi, A., Foldes, A. & Lukacs, B. (2015). Is it time for studying real-life debiasing? Evaluation of the effectiveness of an analogical intervention technique. *Frontiers in Psychology, 6,* 1-13. Accessible at: https://doi.org/10.3389/fpsyg.2015.01120 [downloaded Sept 7, 2018].

Anderson, K. L. (2014). The Effects of Hindsight Bias on Experienced and Inexperienced Auditors' Relevance Ratings of Adverse Factors versus Mitigating Factors. *Journal of Business & Economics Research, 3,* 199-208.

Baer, T., Heiligtag, S. & Samandari, H. (2017). *The business logic in debiasing* [McKinsey & Company]. Accessible at: https://www. mckinsey.com/business-functions/risk/our-insights/the-business-logic-in-debiasing [downloaded Aug 3, 2018].

Bailey, J. A. (2016). *Looking to the Future for Internal Audit Standards: Standards Updates, Usage, and Conformance [CBOK, IIARF].* Accessible at: https://na.theiia.org/iiarf/Pages/CBOK-Research-Resource-Library.aspx [downloaded Aug 4, 2018].

Beller, S. (2016). *Empirisch forschen lernen. Konzepte, Methoden, Fallbeispiele, Tipps [Learn empirically. Concepts, methods, case studies, tips].* Bern, Switzerland: Hogrefe.

Binckli, J. (2014). *"Beauty in the Job" - Physische Attraktivität als sachfremdes Bewerbermerkmal in Personalauswahlverfahren – Eine empirische Untersuchung am Beispiel des universitären Personalauswahlkontextes [Physical Attractiveness as Non-Impact Applicant Feature in Personnel Selection Procedures - An Empirical Study Using the Example of the University Personnel Selection Context],* Diss., Dusseldorf, Germany: Heinrich-Heine-University.

Braun, C., Gründl, M., Marberger, C. & Scherber, C. (2003). Beautycheck. *Ursachen und Folgen von Attraktivität [Causes and consequences of attractiveness].* Accessible at: http://www. beautycheck.de/cmsms/uploads/images/bilder/bericht/beauty_ho_zensi ert.pdf [downloaded Sept 12, 2018].

Bünis, M. & Maruck, A. (2014). Das Berufsbild des Internen Revisors Eine empirische Untersuchung zum aktuellen Entwicklungsstand des kaufmännischen Revisors in Deutschland [The job description of the internal auditor An empirical investigation of the current state of development of the commercial auditor in Germany]. *Zeitschrift Interne Revision*, *5*, 232-241.

Coyne, C. J. & Mathers, R. L. (2011). *The Handbook on the Political Economy of War*. Northampton, USA: Edward Elgar Publishing, Inc.

d'Arcy, A. & Hoos, F. (2012). Welche Faktoren beeinflussen Unabhängigkeit und Objektivität der Internen Revision? Ergebnisse einer Umfrage [Which factors influence the independence and objectivity of Internal Auditing? Results of a survey.]. *Zeitschrift Interne Revision*, *3*, 124-131.

Dion, K., Berscheid, E. & Walster, E. (1972). What is beautiful is good. *Journal of Personality and Social Psychology*, *3*, 285-290.

Dittenhofer, M. A., Evans, R. L., Ramamoorti, S. & Ziegenfuss, D. E. (2011). *Behavioral Dimensions of Internal Auditing: An Exploratory Survey of Internal Auditors*. Altamonte Springs, USA: IIARF.

Downs, A. C. & Lyons, P. M. (1991). Natural observations of the links between attractiveness and initial legal judgments. *Personality and Social Psychology Bulletin*, *5*, 541-547.

D'Onza, G., Sarens, G. & Betti, N. (2016). *Factors enhancing the internal auditing function's ability to add value to the auditees. Evidences from Italian companies* (working paper 2016/05). Accessible at: https://cdn.uclouvain.be/public/Exports%20reddot/ssh-ilsm/images/Betti.pdf [downloaded Sept 5, 2018].

Dunkake, I., Kiechle, T., Klein, M. & Rosar, U. (2012). Schöne Schüler, schöne Noten? Eine empirische Untersuchung zum Einfluss der physischen Attraktivität von Schülern auf die Notenvergabe durch das Lehrpersonal [Beautiful students, nice grades? An empirical study on the influence of students' physical attractiveness on grading by teachers]. *Zeitschrift für Soziologie*, *2*, 142-161.

Earley, C. E., Hoffman, V. B. & Joe, J. R. (2008). Reducing Management's Influence on Auditors' Judgments: An Experimental

Investigation of SOX 404 Assessments. *The Accounting Review*, 6, 1461-1485.

Eulerich, M. & Westhausen, H. U. (2018). Cultural Differences and Similarities between German and Chinese Internal Audit Functions. *Journal of Governance and Regulation*, 2, 2018, 57-73. Accessible at: http://doi.org/10.22495/jgr_v7_i2_p6 [downloaded Sept 4, 2018].

Eulerich, M. (2017). *Enquete 2017.* Die Interne Revision in Deutschland, Österreich und der Schweiz (DIIR, IIRÖ, SVIR) [*Inquete 2017.* The Internal Audit in Germany, Austria and Switzerland (DIIR, IIRÖ, SVIR)].

Eulerich, M., Theis, J. C., Lao, J. & Ramon, M. (2017*). Do fine feathers make a fine bird? The influence of attractiveness on fraud-risk judgments by Internal Auditors.* Accessible at: https://papers.ssrn.com/sol3/papers.cfm?abstract_id=2988269 [downloaded Aug 2, 2018].

Glover, S. M. & Prawitt, D. F. (2012). *Enhancing Board Oversight. Avoiding Judgment Traps and Biases [COSO].* Accessible at: https://www.coso.org/documents/COSO-EnhancingBoardOversight_r8_Web-ready%20%282%29.pdf [downloaded Sept 12, 2018].

Google Scholar. Permanently accessible at: https://scholar.google.de.

Green, W. (2008). Does repetition impair auditors' judgments? *Managerial Auditing Journal*, 8, 724-743.

Guiral, A., Rodgers, W., Ruiz, E. & Gonzalo-Anguloe, J. A. (2015). Can expertise mitigate auditors' unintentional biases? *Journal of International Accounting, Auditing and Taxation*, 24, 105-117.

IIA. (2018). *International Standards for the Professional Practice of Internal Auditing (Standards)* [German edition, version 6.1, Jan 10, 2018]. Frankfurt/M., Germany: DIIR. Accessible at: https://www.diir.de/fileadmin/fachwissen/standards/downloads/IPPF_2017_Standards__Version_6.1___20180110.pdf [downloaded Aug 2, 2018].

Joe, J. R., Vandervelde, S. D. & Wu, Y. J. (2017). Use of High Quantification Evidence in Fair Value Audits: Do Auditors Stay in their Comfort Zone? *The Accounting Review*, 5, 89-116.

Kahneman, D., Rosenfeld, A. M., Gandhi, L. & Blaser, T. (2016). The big Idea – Noise. *Harvard Business Review*, Oct., 38-46.

Kahneman, D., Lovallo, D. & Sibony, O. (2011). Before you make that big decision. *Harvard Business Review*, June, 51-60.

Klein, M. & Rosar, U. (2005). Physische Attraktivität und Wahlerfolg. Eine empirische Analyse am Beispiel der Wahlkreiskandidaten bei der Bundestagswahl 2002 [Physical attractiveness and electoral success. An empirical analysis using the example of constituency candidates in the 2002 Bundestag election]. *Politische Vierteljahresschrift*, *2*, 263-287.

Koch, C., Köhler, A. & Yankova, K. (2016). *Professional skepticism and auditor judgment: Does trait skepticism mitigate the recency bias?* Accessible at: https://papers.ssrn.com/sol3/papers.cfm?abstract_id=2880653 [downloaded Aug 2, 2018].

Kotchetova, N. & Salterio, S. (2009). Judgment and Decision-making Accounting Research: A Quest to Improve the Production, Certification and Use of Accounting Information. In: Koehler. D. J., Harvey, N. (eds.), *Blackwell Handbook of Judgment and Decision Making*, chapter 27, 547-566, Malden, USA: Blackwell.

Langlois, J. H., Kalakanis, L., Rubenstein, A. J., Larson, A., Hallam, M. & Smoot, M. (2000). Maxims or myths of beauty? A meta-analytic and theoretical review. *Psychological Bulletin*, *3*, 390-423.

Larrick, R. P. (2009). Debiasing. In: Koehler. D. J., Harvey, N. (eds.), *Blackwell Handbook of Judgment and Decision Making*, chapter 16, 316-337, Malden, USA: Blackwell.

Lytle, R. D. (2015). *What is Beautiful is Innocent: The Effect of Defendant Physical Attractiveness and Strength of Evidence on Juror Decision-Making.* https://www.researchgate.net/publication/283056488_What_is_Beautiful_is_Innocent_The_Effect_of_Defendant_Physical_Attractiveness_and_Strength_of_Evidence_on_Juror_Decision-Making [downloaded Aug 31, 2018].

Malizia, P., Cannavale, C. & Maimone, F. (2017). *Evolution of the Post-Bureaucratic Organization.* Hershey, USA: IGI Global.

National Commission on the Causes of the financial and economic Crisis in the United States. (2011). *The Financial Crisis Inquiry Report.*

Accessible at: https://www.gpo.gov/fdsys/pkg/GPO-FCIC/pdf/GPO-FCIC.pdf [downloaded Aug 2, 2018].

Nisbett, R. E., Krantz, D. H., Jepson, C. & Kunda, Z. (2013). The Use of Statistical Heuristics in Everyday Inductive Reasoning. In: Gilovich, T., Dale, W. G., Kahneman, D. (eds.), Heuristics and Biases. *The Psychology of Intuitive Judgment*, chapter 28, 510-533, New York, USA: Cambridge University Press.

Palmer, L. A. (2008). Considering Bias in Government Audit Reports – Factors that influence the Judgments of Internal Government Auditors. *Journal of Business Communication, 3,* 265-285.

Paul, R. & Elder, L. (2005). *Critical Thinking Competency Standards. Standards, Principles, Performance Indicators, and Outcomes.* Accessible at: http://www.criticalthinking.org/resources/PDF/CT-competencies%202005.pdf [downloaded Sept 12, 2018].

Rittenberg, L. E. (2016). *Ethics and Pressure: Balancing the Internal Audit Profession [CBOK, IIARF].* Accessible at: https://na.theiia.org/iiarf/Pages/CBOK-Research-Resource-Library.aspx [downloaded Aug 4, 2018].

Rose, J. (2016). *The Top 7 Skills CAEs Want. Building the Right Mix of Talent for Your Organization [CBOK, IIARF].* Accessible at: https://na.theiia.org/iiarf/Pages/CBOK-Research-Resource-Library.aspx [downloaded Sept 12, 2018].

Soll, J. B., Milkman, K. L. & Payne, J. W. (2014). *A User's Guide to Debiasing.* Accessible at: https://faculty.fuqua.duke.edu/~jpayne/bio/working_papers.htm [downloaded Sept 9, 2018].

Stewart, J. & Subramaniam, N. (2010). Internal audit independence and objectivity: emerging research opportunities. *Managerial Auditing Journal, 4,* 328-360.

The Infomaniac. (2018). COGNITIVE BIAS CODEX: 188 Systematic Patterns of Cognitive Deviation; Original DesignHacks.co HI-RES Chart PLUS Individual Quadrants; All Baises Defined (Wikipedia); Referee Logic Infraction Memes. Accessible at: https://throughthe lookingglassnews.wordpress.com/2018/01/05/cognitive-bias-codex-

188-systematic-patterns-of-cognitive-deviation-defined/ [downloaded Aug 2, 2018].

Westhausen, H. U. (2018). Internal Auditing, Psychology and Fraud. In: Columbus, A. M. (ed.), *Advances in Psychology Research*, *133*, 186-209, New York, USA: Nova.

Westhausen, H. U. (2008). Hat sich das Berufsbild der IR in den letzten 5 Jahren verändert? Neuauflage einer empirischen Untersuchung, Soll-Profil und Ausblick [Has the job description of the IR changed in the last 5 years? New edition of an empirical study, target profile and outlook]. *Zeitschrift Interne Revision*, *4*, 172-176.

Wolf, F. (2018). *Accountant and Auditor Bias* [how2ask]. Accessible at: https://www.how2ask.nl/interviewblog/accountant-and-auditor-bias [downloaded Aug 3, 2018].

In: Auditing: An Overview   ISBN: 978-1-53615-116-9
Editors: T. Cavenagh and J. Rymill   © 2019 Nova Science Publishers, Inc.

Chapter 3

ENERGY AUDIT OF WASTE-TO-ENERGY POWER PLANTS

Ali Behbahaninia,[1]***Mohsen Banifateme*[1] *and Sina Azami*[1,2]
[1] Department of Mechanical Engineering,
K. N. Toosi University of Technology, Tehran, Iran
[2] Department of Energy, Politecnico di Torino, Turin, Italy

Abstract

In common energy audition methods, the efficiency of waste-to-energy power plants is evaluated directly. This method is highly sensitive to the measurement errors of waste mass flow which is difficult to be determined precisely. Furthermore, the direct method does not clarify the energy loss sources. Using the indirect method which is proposed in this chapter book, the power plant is split into three sub-systems. These sub-systems are the steam generator, steam cycle and electric generator. The overall efficiency is determined by multiplication of these subsystems' efficiency and taking into account the internal energy usage. The steam generator efficiency is assessed by the loss method. A thermodynamic model was generated in order to evaluate steam cycle efficiency. Electric generator efficiency is estimated by measuring the output power and energy loss terms. Due to fluctuation in the input waste heating value, steam generator and steam cycle parameters are measured iteratively and an averaged value for efficiency is obtained. The method is applied to a waste-to-energy power plant and the efficiency and energy flow diagram are obtained, consequently. The error analysis shows that the present

*Corresponding Author's Email: alibehbahaninia@kntu.ac.ir

method is less sensitive to the mass flow rate of the waste as compared to the direct method.

1. Introduction

Energy audition is an assessment of the energy needs and efficiency of power plants in general. The main target of energy audition is performance estimation of the whole power plant as well as components efficiency and energy loss terms. There are two principal reasons for energy audition of power plants.

(a) Contractual basis: in a contract which is signed between a contractor and a client to construct a new power plant, some parameters such as the power generation, efficiency of whole power system, and air pollution criteria are guaranteed by the contractor. These obligations are checked at the stage of delivering the power plant to the owner through energy audition. This audition is called the "performance test".

(b) Efficiency improvement: usually, power systems and its components are audited regularly to determine energy efficiency of the whole system and each component separately. The efficiency for each component may be compared to results of the test performance to check possible efficiency decline.

Three main parameters are normally required to estimate the efficiency of a power plant that are as follows.

1. Fuel mass rate

2. The fuel heating value

3. Electrical Power generation

The fuel mass flow rate and heating value are measured effortlessly in conventional power plants. In waste-to-energy (WtE) power plants, it is difficult to measure these two parameters. These difficulties not only effect the overall power plant efficiency estimation but also the steam generator audition. A method is presented in detail in this chapter to overcome these difficulties and implemented to an existing WtE power plant. The method determines the plant overall efficiency and also identifies the energy loss terms in different parts of the entire system.

2. Energy Audition of WtE Power Plants

Energy audition method for power systems can be classified into two types. To be more specific, depending on the target industry and the depth to which final audit is needed, an appropriate type of audition is selected. These two types include:

(a) Preliminary audit: in this type of energy audit, the main focus is on visual inspection of the power plant's sections to find probable scopes for energy saving. In addition, it is common to present a number of performance indicators in this way of auditing, namely specific waste consumption (SWC) and overall efficiency (η_o). Consequently, one can obtain how efficient the power plant is working.

(b) Detailed audit: not only the evaluation of all energy using components within the system is covered in this type of energy audit but also it provides a detailed project implementation plan. Besides, the energy flow diagrams illustrated in this step offer the most accurate estimation of energy savings and diagnosis of the sources of losses. In this stage, it is common to suggest some solutions along with economical analysis for more energy saving. It helps auditors to select solutions which are justified from economical view point.

It is worth mentioning that there are a number of standards for energy audition of conventional power plant's main components such as the steam generator, steam turbine and several others that may also be used in WtE power plants. A number of these standards are listed in Table 1. Nevertheless, there are other standards for energy auditing of the power plant's components that are slightly different in terms of required measurement equipment and method of implementation. Depending on plant measurement systems and sensors, an appropriate standard can be utilized for energy audition. Steam generators have been considered as the backbone of power plants due to its significant role. Thus, energy audition of steam generators is the most important step in auditing of the whole power plant. In the case of steam generators in WtE power plant, ASME PTC 34 is the most robust standard that is currently available. In the method presented by this standard, the mass flow rate of the feeding waste is considered to be known and through an iteration procedure, the waste Lower Heating Value (LHV) is calculated. However, the large uncertainty for the waste LHV is the direct result of the inability to measure the weight of the feeding waste accurately.

As explained before there are some problems in energy audition of WtE power plants as listed below:

1. Inlet waste mass flow rate is difficult to measure precisely. This problem is significant in large-scale WtE power plants in which waste is transferred to the WtE power plant via trucks and there is not any other means to evaluate its weight rather than truck scales. Hence, it is required to develop a method that is insensitive to waste mass flow rate fluctuations during working hours of the plant.

2. Waste composition fluctuates and may vary truck by truck whereas the fuel composition in conventional power plants can be considered constant during the test.

3. Many parameters such as pressure and temperature of the steam fluctuate in this kinds of power plants.

The direct method as will be shown in the error analysis section is directly sensitive to the fuel mass flow rate. Moreover, the direct method does not give any information about sources of energy loss terms in the power plant.

Table 1. Components' energy audition list of standards

Component	Standard	Performance indicator
Waste Combustors	ASME PTC 34 (ASME, 2007b)	Efficiency, HHV of waste, Loss terms
Large incinerator	ASME PTC 33 (ASME, 1978)	Efficiency,capacity
Steam Generator	ASME PTC 4.1 (ASME, 2008)	Efficiency, Loss terms
Steam Turbine	ASME PTC 6 (ASME, 1996)	Isentropic efficiency
Centrifugal Pump	ASME PTC 8.2 (ASME, 1990)	Pump efficiency
Air-cooled Steam Condensers	ASME PTC 30.1 (ASME, 2007a)	Capability
Steam Surface Condensers	ASME PTC 12.2 (ASME, 2010)	Overall heat transfer, condenser vacuum
Fans	ASME PTC 11 (ASME, 1984)	Fan efficiency
Closed Feedwater Heaters	ASME PTC 12.1 (ASME, 2000)	Terminal temperature difference(TTD) and Drain cooler(DC)
Ejectors	ASME PTC 24 (ASME, 1976)	Ejector capacity
Deaerators	ASME PTC 12.3 (ASME, 1997)	Terminal temperature difference dissolved oxygen

3. Waste Generation and Management

In recent years, waste generation rates have been growing rapidly worldwide. The disturbing pace of municipal solid waste (MSW) generation trends in any country is directly proportional to population increase, growth in urbanization and industrialization, and growth-centric economy. This is particularly the case in developing countries and the environmental burden continues to be a major issue for them . Comparison of conditions related to MSW management in developed and developing countries brings indicators that quantify the problem.

Similarly, municipal solid waste management (MSWM) has been a considerable challenge to the society. Human activities create waste, and the way these wastes are collected, stored, handled and disposed may pose risks to the environment and to public health. Improper solid waste management has contributed greatly to air, land and water pollution, and to climate change.

3.1. MSW and Its Energy Content

Municipal waste is abundantly available especially in consumer-oriented societies, and is being viewed worldwide as a valuable commodity. It is considerable energy content and high fraction of biogenic carbon (50 – 60 %) indicates high potential as a renewable energy source. Locally generated, waste can be utilized for the recovery of materials and energy rather than disposing in landfills creating environmental hazards (Rada, 2017) (Figure 1).

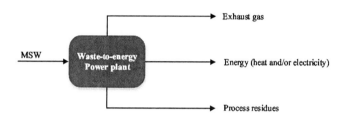

Figure 1. Energy recovery in a waste-to-energy facility.

Energy content of the waste meets the two basic criteria of a renewable energy resource, its fuel source (i.e., municipal solid waste) is sustainable and indigenous. Waste-to-energy facilities generate 'clean' energy from the MSW after some treatment to get the most desirable 'reduce and reuse' of waste. These plants, therefore, can be accounted as any other renewable energy resource. Energy from waste can be a part of a country's energy policy as it present large potential for the mitigation of the negative effects of climate change. The energy content of the waste is expressed as the lower heating value (LHV) which varies widely from country to country. For residual MSW, LHV is about 5–8 MJ/kg in developing countries and 7–10 MJ/kg in industrialized countries (Speight, 2014).

The chemical energy of the waste can be used in diverse energy forms. This process may be done by two main approaches: thermal treatment and biochemical (biological) treatment, as shown in Figure 2. The thermal and biological treatments of waste help basically to divert from landfill large volumes of residual MSW which cannot be economically recycled through materials recovery or through treatment such as composting (Reddy, 2016).

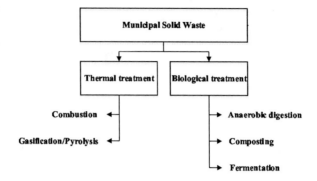

Figure 2. MSW treatment techniques.

4.   Thermal Waste-to-Energy Power Plants

Waste-to-energy plants are designed to incinerate unrecyclable MSW as well as other accepted industrial or commercial waste. They also simultaneously recuperate the energy and remove the pollutants from the eco-cycle thanks to very stringent flue gas cleaning processes.

4.1.   Mass Burning Units

Mass burning WtE power plants are the dominant technology used worldwide for thermal treatment of the MSW. Two techniques are used for burning MSW in mass burning units, distinguished by the degree of fuel preparation. The first technique, known as mass-fired (Figure 3), uses the residue in its as-received, unprepared state. The second burning technique uses prepared residue, or residue-derived fuel (RDF), where the as-received residue is first separated, classified and reclaimed in various ways to yield recyclable products. The remaining material is then shredded and fed into the furnace through multiple feeders onto a traveling grate stoker. Another main difference between the two technologies is the steam generator configuration. Figure 4 illustrate an RDF-fired WtE boiler design developed by the Babcock and Wilcox company (Company, 1913).

Mass burning WtE power plants are normally consists of four main sections:

1. Waste combustion unit

2. Energy recovery unit

3. Energy utilization unit, e.g., turbine, heat

4. Flue gas cleaning units

5. System control and monitoring

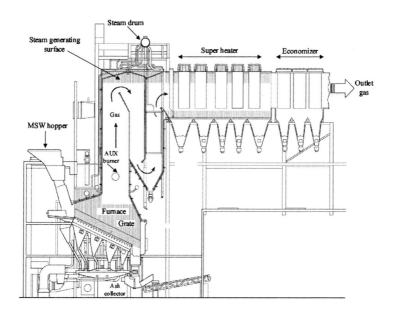

Figure 3. Mass-fired boiler of a mass-burning WtE power plant.

First, the MWS from the pit is fed into the fuel hopper and the grate transports the waste through the combustion chamber. The waste is thus also mixed and burns out completely. Nonburnable material is left as bottom ash at the end of the grate. Metals and construction materials can be recovered from this bottom ash and returned to the material cycle, thereby saving other raw materials and energy that would be used to produce them. Then, The steam generator recovers a great deal of the energy contained in the waste and makes it usable as steam. The energy recovered is therefore usable as electricity and/or heat (e.g., district heating, industrial processes). About half of the energy produced is renewable because it comes from the carbon-neutral biogenic fraction of waste. Finally, Highly sophisticated processes assure that all pollutants contained in the waste and transferred into the flue gas through combustion are eliminated in an efficient, sustainable and reliable way.

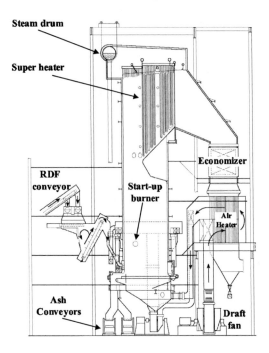

Figure 4. RDF-fired boiler of a mass-burning WtE power plant.

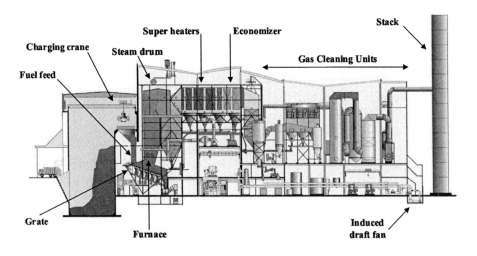

Figure 5. A typical mass-burning WtE power plant.

4.2.   Gasification Integrated WtE Units

Gasification is a process that converts organic (carbonaceous) feedstocks into carbon monoxide, carbon dioxide, and hydrogen by reacting the feedstock at high temperatures ($> 700°C$), without combustion, with a controlled amount of oxygen and/or steam (Ciuta et al., 2017). The resulting gas mixture ,synthesis gas or syngas, is itself a fuel. The power derived from carbonaceous feedstocks and gasification, followed by the combustion of the product gas, is another technology for WtE power plants.

As it is illustrated in Figure 6, a gasification integrated WtE power plant system consists of the following process stages:

1. Fuel preparation

2. Thermal conversion (gasification and oxidation)

3. Heat recovery steam generator and power cycle

4. Flue gas cleaning units

5. System control and monitoring

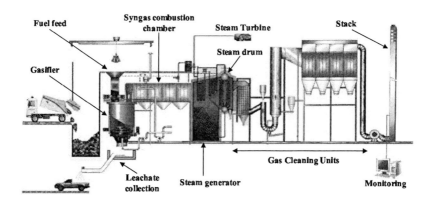

Figure 6. A typical gasification integrated WtE power plant.

Feeding waste utilised in these plants is normally to be pre-treated prior to use, which involves shredding the waste and magnetically separating ferrous materials which can be recycled. The pre-treated waste (fuel) is then stored in a fuel bunker, and gasification chamber is fed via a fuel-hopper with an automatic crane system. The air from the reception hall is used as process air for the gasification process, this creates a slight negative pressure in the reception hall and eliminates odor. The thermal conversion is carried in two stages:

- **Primary Chamber** where gasification of the waste takes place to produce a synthetic gas.

- **Secondary Chamber** where the synthetic gas is oxidized at a high temperature.

This highly controlled two-stage process enables a simple dry flue gas treatment system to be employed and eliminates the need for a sophisticated and costly end of pipe flue-gas treatment system.

Then, hot flue gas from the secondary chamber is recovered in the Heat Recovery Steam Generator (HRSG) section of the plant. The HRSG consists of a water-tube boiler, a super heater and an economizer. The steam generated in this section is used in a single-drum Rankine cycle to run an steam turbine.

The flue gas cleaning units are mainly consists of activated carbon columns, acid scrubbers and PTFE filters. Before entering the stack, the outlet gas should be monitored with accuracy in order to guarantee that it meets the the environmental protection agency (EPA) limitations.

4.3. Gasification WtE Units with Internal Combustion Engine (ICE)

These plants are mainly distinguished by their power cycle which runs by reciprocating engines rather than steam turbine. Therefore, the HRSG section is eliminated, but a syngas cooling system is added to decrease the produced gas temperature before entering the gas cleaning units (Luque and Speight, 2014). The system is consists of 5 basic sections that are shown in Figure 7. These sections are listed as below:

1. Fuel preparation unit

2. Gasification

3. Syngas cleaning units

4. Syngas combustion in an ICE

5. Continuous emissions monitoring system (CEMS)

MSW treatment in this technology is highly crucial as it is directly influences the quality of produced syngas, and it is consists of a shredder set, a planetary mixer and briquetting machine. The prepared fuel is formed into pellets, which ensures stable

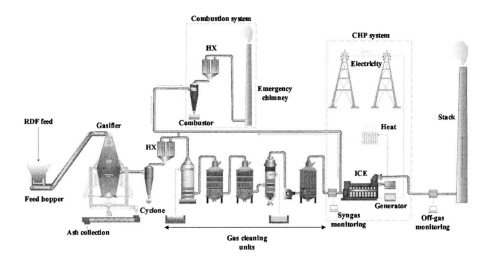

Figure 7. A typical gasification-ICE integrated WtE power plant.

operation of the gasification reactor. The advantage of this approach is the fact that, it ensures a continuous fuel transportation to the gasifier and restricts the amount of residual air in the porous structures of the materials.

Gasification is carried out by a movable segmented grate in commercial units. Gasifying agent is air, whereas the energy efficiency in terms of energy conversion of formed fuel / syngas amounts up to 80 %. Furthermore, low temperature gasification process minimizes the production of slag, whereas the innovative use of thermal energy recycling guarantees process stability and quality of the syngas.

The syngas purification system plays an important role in the entire technology line. This is due to the need to meet very strict quality requirements for the permissible amount of pollutants, especially when fed to internal combustion engines. Syngas treatment consists of:

- • – separation of tars through a cooling system and two-stage filtration

- • – separation of acidic gases through absorption

- • – thorough cleaning and stabilization of the syngas quality through adsorption

This unit is composed by a highly efficient cogeneration system - internal combustion engine with a catalyst, generator and a combined heat and power (CHP) system. Finally, The flue gases from the syngas combustion process in the engine will be discharged to the emitter. A continuous measurement of the quality of the process is provided in terms of fuel composition formed, the composition of syngas at various stages of production and the quality of exhaust gas. The scope for continuous emissions monitoring of flue gases includes all pollutants which are required to be monitored in syngas combustion plants.

5.   Methodology and Computations

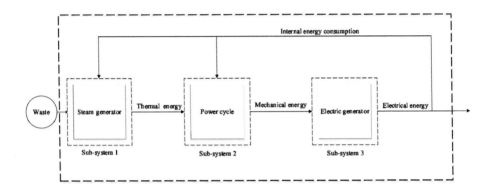

Figure 8. Schematic of WtE systems and their subsystems.

Schematic of a typical WtE power plant is presented in Figure 8. As it can be seen, the whole system may be split into three main sub-systems. First, the waste enters to sub-system 1 which is the steam generator. This sub-system contains a boiler in case of mass burning power plants or a gasifier and a combustion chamber followed by a heat recovery steam generator (HRSG) in gasification integrated WtE power plants. Hence, sub-system 1 converts the chemical energy of the waste to the thermal energy. The second sub-system is the power cycle in which the thermal energy is converted to the mechanical energy through an steam turbine. Thereafter, the mechanical energy is converted to electrical energy in sub-system 3, the electric generator. A portion of this electricity is then reused in the pumps, fans and the other electrical components within the WtE system, and the rest is the net electricity production delivered to the grid.

5.1.   Direct Method

In direct method, the efficiency of a power plant is calculated by using the following equation.

$$\eta = \frac{3412 \times (TGE - IEC)}{M_f LHV_f + M_{af} LHV_{af}} \tag{1}$$

TGE: Total generator electricity production.

IEC: Internal electricity consumption.

M_f: Mass of waste dispose

LHV_f: Lower heating value of waste

M_{af}: Mass of auxiliary fuel consumption

LHV_{af}: Lower heating value of auxiliary fuel

To overcome the uncertainty due to fluctuation in the heating value of the waste and errors in measuring the mass flow rate of the waste, it is recommended to measure net power generation of the power plant and mass of the waste in a long-enough period of time. LHV of the waste is determined by an iterative sampling procedure and averaging through this period of time.

The direct method as will be explained in the error analysis section is directly sensitive to the waste mass flow rate. Moreover, the direct method does not give any information about sources of energy loss terms within the WtE power plant. The measured data required for the direct method is shown in Table 2.

Table 2. List of parameters to be measured for the direct method

No	Symbol	Definition	Unit
1	TGE	Total generator electricity production	kWh
2	IEC	Internal electricity consumption	kWh
3	M_f	Mass of waste dispose	lb
4	LHV_f	Lower heating value of waste	Btu/lb
5	M_{af}	Mass of auxiliary fuel consumption	lb
6	LHV_{af}	Lower heating value of auxiliary fuel	Btu/lb

5.2. Indirect Method

In the proposed method in this chapter, the steam generator, steam cycle and eclectic generator efficiencies are evaluated separately. The overall efficiency is then determined by multiplication of these three efficiencies, taking into account the internal energy consumption. The steam generator efficiency is defined based on a similar procedure presented in ASME PTC 4.1 (ASME, 2008).

The Rankine cycle efficiency is resulted from thermodynamic simulation of the cycle. The steam cycle main parameters may fluctuate in the time of audition therefore an averaged value may be used in this method. The efficiency of the electric generator may be estimated based on measurements or the reported value in power plant documents. The fourth term is considered for internal electricity consumption of the WtE plant.

As it can be seen in equation 2, the overall efficiency is equal to the multiplication of the efficiency of sub-systems 1 to 3 and the term relating to the internal electricity consumption.

$$\eta_o = \eta_1 . \eta_2 . \eta_3 \left(1 - \frac{IEC}{TGE} \right) \tag{2}$$

η_o: Overall system efficiency

η_1: Efficiency of steam generator

η_2: Efficiency of power cycle

η_3: Efficiency of electric generator

TGE: Total generator electricity production

IEC: Internal electricity consumption

Inspecting equation 2, the waste mass flow has appeared only in steam generator efficiency calculation. In the current approach, the steam generator efficiency is estimated by loss method. since, loss method efficiency is assessed by subtracting the normalized values of the loss terms from 100 %. Again, in many of these loss terms waste mass flow rate is eliminated. Therefore, the method is almost insensitive to errors in the waste mass flow.

5.2.1. Steam Generator

There are also two methods to evaluate steam generators efficiency, the direct and loss method. Loss method for efficiency estimation of conventional steam boilers is described in ASME PTC 4.1. Similarly, loss method for energy audition of heat recovery steam generators is presented in ASME PTC 4.4 (ASME, 1981). Same methods have been presented for these components in other standards and source-books. Loss method for waste-to-energy boilers is presented in ASME PTC 34. It is worth to note that different approaches may be used by auditors due to measurement limitations. The presented method is different from the method described in the ASME PTC 34 in many aspects. In ASME PTC 34 uncertainty of waste mass flow rate has been ignored completely and the boiler is used as a calorimeter to estimate the heating value of the waste. In the proposed method, LHV of the waste is determined by sampling and averaging of the input waste. Besides, the method is almost insensitive to the waste mass flow rate uncertainty. Finally, the control volume used in the current method (CV1) on the contrary to the ASME PTC 34 (CV2) includes the waste pit; therefore, a term for leachate is added to the loss termss as illustrated in Figure 9.

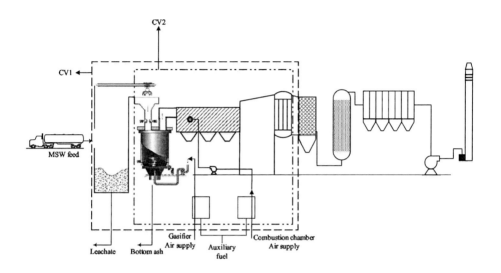

Figure 9. Control volumes imposed on sub-system 1.

Heat balance diagram of the steam generator in the proposed loss method is presented in Figure 10. Eleven loss terms are defined. The first three terms are stack sensible and latent heat loss terms. Loss due to incomplete combustion is calculated through Q_4 and Q_5. Q_6 presents sensible heat loss by the residue. Q_7 is representative of the radiation heat loss term. Q_8 is the chemical energy loss due to leachate disposal from the waste pit. Q_9 is the heat loss by water or steam enters in the gas side of the steam generator. Q_{10} is a loss term of steam injected in air preheater coil and Q_{11} take place when cooling water removes energy from the steam generator. It should be noted that all energy loss terms are calculated per mass of the feeding waste.

The analysis of waste, flue gas, and measurement of the steam generator output temperature was carried out several times and the average values were used to calculate the steam generator efficiency. The measuring data for audition of steam generator is presented in Table 3.

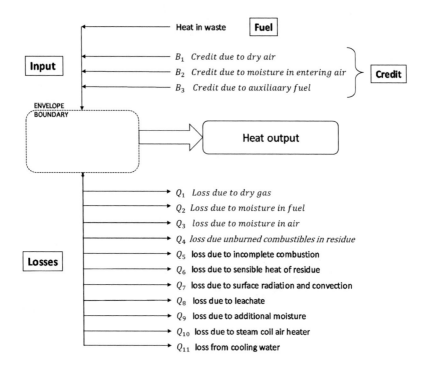

Figure 10. Heat balance of the steam generator.

Energy Losses

Q_1: Energy Loss Due to Flue Gas

There is an energy loss associated with sensible heat of the dry flue gas leaving the steam generator with the higher temperature than the reference temperature. Q_1 depends directly on the mass flow rate of the dry flue gas. Generally, there are two methods to estimate the mass flow rate. ASME PTC 34 suggests that the mass flow rate is calculated by taking a control volume around the economizer. This method is applied in case there are temperature sensors to determine the inlet and outlet streams temperature. In this chapter, mass flue rate of the dry flue gas per mass of the waste is calculated in terms of the flue gas analysis as presented in equation 4.

$$Q_1 = W_{dg}.H_{fg} \qquad (3)$$

H_{fg}: Enthalpy of dry flue gas leaving conrol volume (CV1) and calculated by methods of ASME(ASME, 2008)

Table 3. List of parameters to be measured for steam generators

Symbol	Description	Unit	Method of measurement
$\dot{m}_f$	Mass flow rate of waste	lb/hr	Section 7.3.
$\dot{m}_a$	Mass flow rate of air inlet	lb/hr	section 8.1.
$\dot{m}_r$	Mass flow rate of residue	lb/hr	Section 7.4.
$\dot{m}_l$	Mass flow rate of leachate	lb/hr	Section 7.5.
$\dot{m}_{af}$	Mass flow rate of auxiliary fuel	lb/hr	Mass flow meter
O_2	Volume percent in dry flue gas	Percent	Gas analyzer
CO_2	Volume percent in dry flue gas	Percent	Gas analyzer
CO	Volume percent in dry flue gas	Percent	Gas analyzer
T_g	Temperature of flue gas outlet	$°F$	Thermometer
T_a	Temperature of air inlet	$°F$	Thermometer
T_r	Temperature of residue outlet	$°F$	Thermometer
T_{rv}	Temperature of references	$°F$	standard
LHV_f	Lower heating value of waste	Btu/lb	section 7.2.
LHV_{af}	Lower heating value of auxiliary fuel	Btu/lb	calorimeter
m_{wf}	Percentage of moisture in waste	lb/lb	Waste analysis
$(H_2O)_l$	Percentage of moisture in leachate	lb/lb	Laboratory
ω	Absolute humidity	lb/lb	Psychrometric
C	Percentage of carbon in waste	lb/lb	Laboratory
C_r	Percentage of carbon in residue	lb/lb	Laboratory
C_l	Percentage of carbon in leachate	lb/lb	Laboratory
H	Percentage of hydrogen in waste	lb/lb	Laboratory
S	Percentage of sulfur in waste	lb/lb	Laboratory

W_{dg}: Mass of dry flue gas per mass of waste which is calculated as follows (ASME, 1964).

$$W_{dg} = \frac{11CO_2 + 8O_2 + 7(CO + N_2)}{3(CO_2 + CO)} \times C_b + \left[\frac{12.01S}{32.07}\right] \qquad (4)$$

CO_2: Volume percent of Carbon dioxide in flue gas

N_2: Volume percent of nitrogen in flue gas

O_2: Volume percent of oxygen in flue gas

S: Mass percentage of sulfur in waste

C_b: Amount of burnt carbon per mass of waste which is calculated using equation 5.

$$C_b = C - C_r.W_r - C_l.W_l \qquad (5)$$

C: Mass percentage of carbon in waste

W_r: Mass of residue per mass of waste

C_r: Mass percentage of carbon in residue

W_l: Mass of leachate per mass of waste

C_l: Mass percentage of carbon in leachate

$$H_{fg} = MCP_{fg}\,(T_g - 77) \qquad (6)$$

T_g: outlet temperature of flue gas

MCP_{fg}: Mean specific heat of flue gas

Q_2: Energy Loss Due to Moisture in the Waste

The feeding waste enters the pit contains some degrees of moisture. A portion of this moisture leaves the pit by leachate disposal. Besides, H_2O is formed due to the reaction of H_2 content of the waste and inlet air to the control volume. The moisture is then vaporized and leaves the HRSG with the stack temperature. The loss associated with the moisture is calculated as follows.

$$Q_2 = m_{vfg} * (H_v - H_{Rv}) \qquad (7)$$

m_{vfg}: Mass of moisture in flue gas per mass of waste (ASME, 1964)

H_v: Enthalpy of water vapor at 1 psi and T_g

T_g : Outlet temperature of flue gas

H_{Rv}: Enthalpy of water at reference temperature

$$m_{vfg} = 8.936H + m_{wf} - m_{wl} \qquad (8)$$

H: Mass percentage of hydrogen in waste

m_{wf}: Mass percentage of moisture in waste

m_{wl}: Mass of water in leachate per mass of waste and is calculated using equation 9

$$m_{wl} = (H_2O)_l * W_l \tag{9}$$

W_l: Mass of leachate per mass of waste

$(H_2O)_l$: Mass percentage of moisture in leachate

Q_3: Energy Loss Due to Moisture in Air

The humid incoming air is superheated as it passes through the steam generator and the water content is vaporized due to the high temperature. To relate this loss to the mass of waste, the moisture content of the inlet air and the amount of air supplied per mass of waste burnt must be known. This loss can be derived as below.

$$Q_3 = \omega.W_a.H_{va} \tag{10}$$

ω: Absolute humidity

W_a: Mass of inlet air per mass of waste

H_{va}: Enthalpy of water vapor at T_g which is calculated using steam table

Q_4: Energy Loss Due to Unburned Combustibles in Residue

Some carbon is left unburned in residue. Associated energy loss to this unburned carbon is calculated as follows.

$$Q_4 = W_r.C_r.LHV_c \tag{11}$$

W_r: Mass of residue per mass of waste

C_r: Mass percentage of carbon in residue

LHV_c: Lower heating value of carbon

in which LHV_c equals to 12000 Btu/lb.

Q_5: Energy Loss Due to Incomplete Combustion

Complete combustion of any hydrocarbon forms CO_2. Carbon monoxide is formed due to incomplete combustion. Carbon monoxide concentration may measure easily by flue gas analyzer. Loss term associated with formation of CO is calculated as follows.

$$Q_5 = CO.W_{dg}.LHV_{co}\frac{Mw_{co}}{Mw_{fg}} \tag{12}$$

CO: Volume fraction of Carbon monoxide in flue gas

W_{dg}: Mass of dry flue gas per mass of waste Which is calculated using equation 4

Mw_{co}: Molecular weight of carbon monoxide

MW_{fg}: Molecular weight of flue gas

LHV_{co}: Lower heating value of carbon monoxide

in which MW_{co} equals to 28.01 lb/lbmol and LHV_{co} equals to 4336.89 Btu/lb. Flue gas molecular weight is defined as:

$$MW_{fg} = 28.01CO + 44.01CO_2 + 16O_2 + 28.01N_2 \tag{13}$$

CO_2: Volume percent of Carbon dioxide in flue gas

CO: Volume percent of Carbon monoxide in flue gas

N_2: Volume percent of nitrogen in flue gas

O_2: Volume percent of oxygen in flue gas

Q_6: Energy Loss Due to Sensible Heat of Residue

The residue leaves the control volume at a temperature above the reference temperature. The heat loss can be obtained as follows.

$$Q_6 = W_r.H_r \tag{14}$$

W_r: Residue mass per waste mass

H_r: Enthalpy of residue at T_r which is calculated as follows (ASME, 2008)

$$H_r = MCP_r(T_r - 77) \tag{15}$$

T_r: Temperature of residue leaving control volume (CV1)

MCP_r: Mean specific heat of residue

Q_7: Energy Loss Due to Surface Radiation and Convection

This parameter is calculated via the following equations (Sewa Bhawan, 2010):

$$Q_7 = \frac{q \times A}{\dot{m}_f} \tag{16}$$

$$q_i = 0.174 \left[\left(\frac{T_{si} + 460}{100} \right)^4 - \left(\frac{T_o + 460}{100} \right)^4 \right] + 0.296 \left(T_{si} - T_o \right)^{1.25} \sqrt{\left(\frac{196.85 V_m + 68.9}{68.9} \right)} \tag{17}$$

A_i: Surface area hrsg, gasifier and combustion chamber

T_{si}: Average surface temperature of hrsg, gasifier and combustion chamber

V_m: Velocity of wind

However, Q_7 can be approximated by the radiation and convection loss charts presented in different standards and technical manuals.

Q_8: Energy Loss Due to Leachate

Energy loss due to leachate leaving the CV1 is obtained by equation 18.

$$Q_8 = W_l . C_l LHV_c \tag{18}$$

W_l: Mass of leachate per mass of waste

C_l: Mass percentage of carbon in leachate

LHV_c: Lower heating value of carbon

in which LHV_c equals to 12000 Btu/lb.

Q_9: Energy Loss Due to Additional Moisture

In some mass burning WtE power plant additional water or steam may be introduced to the system in order to control the temperature of the furnace. This moisture content must be treated separately from the total water from fuel and inlet air.

$$Q_9 = \frac{\dot{m}_f}{\dot{m}_{Am}} \left(H_s - H_{Rv} \right) \tag{19}$$

$\dot{m}_f$: Mass flow rate of waste

$\dot{m}_{Am}$: Mass flow rate of additional moisture

H_s: Enthalpy of steam at outlet flue gas temperature

H_{Rv}: Enthalpy of water at reference temperature

Q_{10}: Energy Loss Due to Steam Coil Air Heater When Steam Source is From Boiler

The steam generated in the boiler may be used in steam coil air heater which is responsible to preheat the air entering steam generator. The loss is the product of the condensate flow from the air preheater coil and the difference in enthalpy of the condensate and entering feed-water. The condensate flow should not be included in the boiler output.

$$Q_{10} = \frac{\dot{m}_{wsa}}{\dot{m}_f} \left(H_{vi} - H_{we} \right) \tag{20}$$

$\dot{m}_{wsa}$: Mass flow rate of steam consumption in steam coil air heater

$\dot{m}_f$: Mass flow rate of waste

H_{vi}: Enthalpy of steam consumption in steam coil air heater

H_{we}: Enthalpy of water at outlet of steam coil air heater

Q_{11}: Energy Loss from Cooling Water

This energy loss associated with the cooling water that removes energy from the steam generator CV1. this loss can be shown as follows.

$$Q_{11} = \frac{\dot{m}_{cw}}{\dot{m}_f} \left(H_{cwe} - H_{cwi} \right) \tag{21}$$

$\dot{m}_{cw}$: Mass flow rate of cooling water

$\dot{m}_f$: Mass flow rate of waste

H_{cwi}: Enthalpy of water at inlet water for cooling

H_{cwe}: Enthalpy of water at outlet water for cooling

Credits

Credit terms present inlet energy to the steam generator other than the waste and supplementary fuel.

B_1: Credit Due to Dry Air

Dry air entering the combustion chamber or the gasifier may have temperature above the reference temperature. Energy input to the system envelope due to this elevated temperature can be considered as below.

$$B_1 = W_a.H_{ai} \tag{22}$$

W_a: Mass of dry air per mass of waste

H_{ai}: Enthalpy of dry air at the average air temperature entering the steam generator wich is calculated by equation 24 (ASME, 2008)

If there are several (n) air inlets, average temperature calculated as follows (ASME, 2007b).

$$T_A = \frac{\dot{m}_{a1}.T_{a1} + \dot{m}_{a2}.T_{a2} + ... + \dot{m}_{an}.T_{an}}{M_a} \tag{23}$$

$\dot{m}_a$: Total mass flow rate of inlet air

$\dot{m}_{an}$: Mass flow rate of inlet air at n

T_{an}: Temperature of inlet air at n

$$H_{ai} = MCP_{ai}(T_A - 77) \tag{24}$$

T_A: Temperature of Air inlet

MCP_{ai}: Mean specific heat of dry air at T_A

B_2: Credit Due to Moisture in Entering Dry Air

The moisture content within the entering air to the system may also add an energy credit to the assumed envelope. This credit presented in equation 25.

$$B_2 = \omega.W_a.H_{wa} \tag{25}$$

ω: Absolute humidity

W_a: Mass of dry air per mass of waste

H_{wa}: Enthalpy of water vapor at T_A which is calculated using steam table

B_3: Credit Due to Auxiliary Fuel

Energy input relating to the auxiliary fuel is obtained from the following equation.

$$B_4 = \frac{\dot{m}_{af}}{\dot{m}_f} \cdot LHV_{af} \tag{26}$$

$\dot{m}_{af}$: Mass of auxiliary fuel consumption

$\dot{m}_f$: Mass of waste

LHV_{af}: Lower heating value of auxiliary fuel

Calculated Efficiency

Energy loss terms is derived by dividing each losses by the summation of LHV of the waste and credits.

$$L_i = \frac{Q_i}{LHV_f + \sum_{i=1}^{4} B_i} \tag{27}$$

Q_i: Heat losses

LHV_f: Lower heating value of waste

B_i: Credits

Consequently, the steam generator efficiency can be obtained by subtracting the loss terms from 1.

$$\eta = 1 - \sum_{i=1}^{11} L_i \tag{28}$$

5.2.2. Power Cycle

The dominant technology used in WtE power plants is based on steam generation which runs a Rankine cycle. The steam is used as working medium follows the Rankine cycle and produce power via steam turbines. The WtE power cycles usually use a single drum HRSG with one extraction from the turbine that feeds a deaerator. Besides, a condensate pump and a boiler feed pump are necessities in every WtE power cycles. A

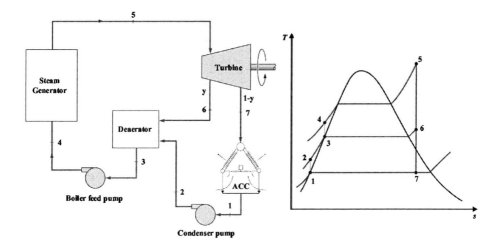

Figure 11. Main components of a WtE power cycle and the representing T-S diagram.

simple scheme of the power cycle as well as the cycle representation on T-S diagram is shown in Figure 11.

Power plant engineers and specialists are interested in a efficiency as a term of the economy of the power plant, since it has an effect on capital, fuel, and operating costs. In addition, another parameter that more readily reflects the fuel economy is called heat rate (HR). It is the amount of heat added, often in Btu, to produce a unit amount of work in kWh. Therefore, heat rate has the units Btu/kWh. There are various heat rates corresponding to the work used in the denominator. A number of definitions for HR is listed below:

$$Net\ cycle\ HR = \frac{rate\ of\ heat\ added\ to\ cycle}{net\ cycle\ power} \qquad (29)$$

$$Gross\ cycle\ HR = \frac{rate\ of\ heat\ added\ to\ cycle}{turbine\ power\ output} \qquad (30)$$

$$Net\ station\ HR = \frac{rate\ of\ heat\ added\ to\ steam\ generator}{net\ station\ power} \qquad (31)$$

$$Gross\ station\ HR = \frac{rate\ of\ heat\ added\ to\ steam\ generator}{gross\ turbine\ generator\ power\ output} \qquad (32)$$

$$HR = \frac{3412}{\eta_{th}} \qquad (33)$$

As it is shown in Figure 8, internal consumption of fans and pumps are taking into account in a separate term called internal energy usage; therefore, gross cycle heat rate equation 30 is used to calculate the thermal efficiency of the power cycle.

in order to implement a complete an accurate energy audit of the power cycle, pressure and temperature of different points of the power cycle should be read from power plant sensors. Finally, the simulation of the power cycle is conducted based on the gathered data.

Energy Auditing of Steam Turbines

In order to simulate steam Rankine cycle, it is required to know the steam turbine isotropic efficiency. Moreover, the steam turbine auditing is considered to be one of the most important steps in any audition program regarding steam power plants. Within the turbine, the energy level of the working fluid goes on decreasing along the flow stream. The main standard regarding steam turbines energy audition is ASME PTC 6. The isentropic efficiency of the steam turbine can be calculated as follows and list of input parameter for auditing of steam turbine are brought in Table 4.

$$\eta_s = \frac{h_{in} - h_{out}}{h_{in} - h_{out,s}} \tag{34}$$

h_{in}: Enthalpy of steam entering the turbine

h_{out}: Enthalpy of steam leaving the turbine

$h_{out,s}$: Enthalpy of steam isentropic process at the turbine exit

Table 4. List of parameters to be measured for steam turbines audition

Symbol	Definition	Unit
h_{in}	Enhalpy of steam entering the turbine	Btu/lb
h_{out}	Enhalpy of steam leaving the turbine	Btu/lb
$h_{out,s}$	Enhalpy of steam isentropic process at the turbine excite	Btu/lb

The outlet steam from an steam turbine is typically in the super-heated area, which in this case, its enthalpy can be obtained by its pressure and temperature.

On the other hand, if the outlet steam is in the liquid-vapor region, a proper sensor is needed to indicate the steam quality. The enthalpy can also be calculated by applying the first law of thermodynamics for the turbine, according to the procedure presented in ASME PTC 6.

The first law of thermodynamics for the turbine is defined as follows (Figure 13). It should be noted that $\dot{W}_{shaft}$ is calculated from equation 64, in section 6.

$$\sum \dot{m}_{in} h_{in} = \sum \dot{m}_{out} h_{out} + \sum \dot{m}_{ext} h_{ext} + \dot{W}_{shaft} \qquad (35)$$

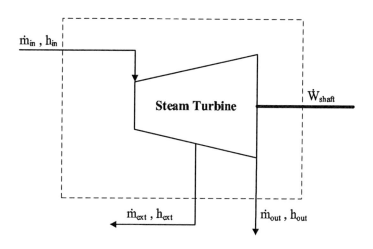

Figure 12. Scheme of a turbine inlet and outlet streams.

Energy Auditing of Pumps

Generally, there are two main pumps in a steam cycle, condenser pump that increases pressure of the feedwater from the condenser to the deaerator pressure and boiler feed pump that increases the feedwater pressure from the dearator to the steam generator. Similar to the steam turbine, efficiency of the pump is required to model the steam cycle, hence, pumps must be audited in a regular steam cycle energy audition.

Input parameters for energy audition of pump are brought in Table 5.

$$\eta_{pump} = \frac{P_h}{P_T} \qquad (36)$$

P_h: Hydraulic power and is calculated using equation 37

P_T: Power input to the pump

$$P_h = Q \left(h_d - h_s\right) \rho g \qquad (37)$$

Q: Volume flow rate of pump

$(h_d - d_s)$: Head of pump

ρ: Density of water

g: Gravitational acceleration

Table 5. List of parameters to be measured for pumps audition

Symbol	Definition	Unit
P_{in}	Inlet flow pressure to pump	psia
P_{out}	Outlet flow pressure of pump	psia
ρ	Density of flow	lbm/ft^2
Q	Volume flow rate of pump	ft^3/sec

5.2.3. Electric Generator

An electric generator is a device that converts mechanical energy into electrical power that is transferred in the electricity grid. The first law of thermodynamics is applied to a generator as it is illustrated in Figure 13.

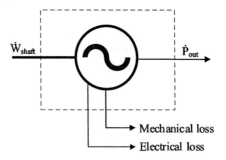

Figure 13. Electric generator's inlet and outlet streams.

$$\dot{W}_{shaft} = \dot{P}_{out} + [Q_{mech} + Q_{el}] \tag{38}$$

Table 6. List of parameters to be measured for electric generators

Symbol	Definition	Unit
TGE	Total generator electricity production	kWh
IEC	Internal electricity consumption	kWh
Q_{mech}	Mechanical loss	kWh
Q_{el}	Electrical loss	kWh

$\dot{W}_{shaft}$: Shaft work

$\dot{P}_{out}$: Output electericity

Q_{mech}: Mechanical loss

Q_{el}: Electerical loss

$$\dot{P}_{out} = TGE - IEC \tag{39}$$

Consequently, the efficiency of the generator (η_{gen}) is obtained from the following equation:

$$\eta_{gen} = 1 - \frac{Q_{mech} + Q_{el}}{\dot{W}_{shaft}} \tag{40}$$

The main parameters for energy audit of generator are brought in Table 6.

6. Another Definition for Energy Efficiency

In the methodology described in section 5., CV1 in Figure 8 was used to define the energy efficiency of the steam generator. In the method presented in ASME PTC 34, CV2 was defined as the boundary of the steam generator.

Due to the difficulties in measuring the heating value of the waste at the boundary of the CV2 in Figure 8, the method presented in ASME PTC 34 somehow considers the steam generator as a calorimeter to estimate the heating value of the waste. The present method may be modified in a way, so that the efficiency is defined similar to the ASME PTC 34.

Thus, the waste pit is considered within a control volume and mass/energy balance is applied to it, as illustrated in Figure 14.

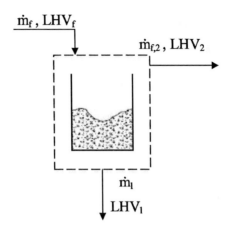

Figure 14. Control volume imposed on a waste pit.

$$\dot{m}_{f,2} = \dot{m}_f - \dot{m}_l \tag{41}$$

$$\dot{m}_{f,2} LHV_2 = \dot{m}_f LHV_f - \dot{m}_l LHV_l \tag{42}$$

To do so, one can change the parameters $\dot{m}_f$ and LHV_f with $M_{f,2}$ and LHV_2, and remove the leachate from loss terms. Then, apply the proposed method based on new data.

7. Measurement

The list of parameters to measure is presented in previous sections, but in this section, the measurement techniques and methods are covered in detail.

7.1. Waste Sampling

Incinerators may receive a wide variety of materials, the moisture content of which are higher than the air-dried level. This heterogeneity and moisture content complicate both the size and number of increments that must be taken, as well as the reduction of the sample to represent amounts that can be analyzed. In all cases, the incoming waste must be adequately mixed before sampling with precautions taken to prevent density segregation. If the waste is processed (shredded and classified), care must be taken to ensure a representative sample reflecting the fuel waste composition to the incineration system.

7.2.   LHV of Waste

The LHV can be defined through an iterative sampling of the waste from the waste pit and putting the sample inside a bomb calorimeter. Thereafter, the gathered data were analyzed statistically and the error distribution plots were derived accordingly. As a result, the LHV of the waste is determined in numbers with its uncertainty.

Additionally, numerous equations were proposed to calculate the LHV of solid fuels according to the fuel's ultimate analysis ($wt\%$). However, it is worth mentioning that a large uncertainty for the waste fuel LHV may occur if one apply these equations. Hence, the authors suggest to follow the experimental sampling process.

7.3.   Waste Mass Flow Measurement

One of the difficulties in the audition of WtE power plants is the waste mass flow rate measurement. Methods to measure this parameter and its associated uncertainty is described in ASME PTC 34 in detail. There are two methods to estimate the waste mass flow rate:

1. Crane scale: in this method, the crane scale system must be calibrated first. This calibration consists of conveying a known weight by the crane. The measured value by this method is slightly different with the truck method due to the weight of leachate exiting the control volume.

2. Truck scale: in this method, the waste pit level must be the same at the end and start of the audition.

7.4.   Mass Flow Rate of Residue

The amount of residue leaving the WtE envelope is required to determine the heat losses associated with the residue streams. Residue streams that leave the system (cross the CV1) may include bottom ash, boiler ash or fly ash.

The amount of residue must be separated, gathered, and weighed for the test period if it is practical to do so. If the residue is cooled in water basin, the residue should be weighed wet and the moisture content subtracted from the total weight to calculated the dry weight.

7.5. Mass Flow Rate of Leachate

Generally, leachate is transferred into a storage pool in the WtE power plants. The mass flow rate of leachate is calculated daily due to the height changes in the pool, and by repeating and averaging the obtained value, the mass flow rate of leachate is estimated for further calculations.

7.6. Other Measurements

The composition of flue gas was obtained by the gas analyzer. The temperature of the various points was measured with the appropriate sensors in the power plant. The composition of the waste, residue, and leachate was determined by testing in the laboratory that consequently gives the approximate and ultimate analysis of the waste.

For power cycle components, measurements were performed by means of numerous sensors and can be monitored in the power plant's control room, so a number of the required data were extracted from there.

It is to be noted that to determine the amount of electricity produced and the amount of internal electricity consumption, the data from the control room of the power plant were used.

8. Energy Audition of Other Components

There are some other components in WtE power plants that may be audited by similar methods used to audit conventional power plants. The main scope of this chapter is to develop a method for energy audition of WtE power plants; therefore, audition of these components is discussed in brief.

8.1. Fans

Fans are considered to be major energy consumption components in air-cooled condensers, gasification reactors, and WtE furnaces. Energy audition of fans is covered in ASME PTC 11. The efficiency of a fan may be estimated as follows:

$$\eta = \frac{Q.\Delta P}{C.P_{sh}} \tag{43}$$

In which, C depends on units of measurement and P_{sh} is the power input to the shaft. This power input may be evaluated directly by a torque meter and a tachometer.

The volumetric flow may be estimated by the following equation:

$$Q = \overline{V}A \tag{44}$$

To obtain an average velocity inside the duct, velocity must be measured at a series of equal points with the equal area (Figure 15).

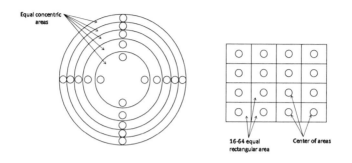

Figure 15. Measurement points on round and square duct areas.

8.2. Air-Cooled Condenser

A detail performance estimation of air-cooled condensers (ACC) is brought in ASME PTC 30.1. The capability is describing the performance of an ACC and it is defined from equation 45.

$$C = 100 \frac{\dot{m}_{S,T}}{\dot{m}_{S,G}} \tag{45}$$

In which, $\dot{m}_{S,T}$ is guaranteed mass flow rate and $\dot{m}_{S,G}$ is the test mass flow rate corrected for steam quality, ambient pressure, fan motor power, inlet air temperature and turbine back pressure.

8.3. Feedwater Heaters

Closed feedwater heaters are used in the high-pressure steam cycle to preheat water entering steam generator by extracted steam from the turbine. Generally, closed feedwater heaters are rarely used in WtE power plants because WtE power plants usually have lower HRSG pressure with respect to conventional steam power plants. Temperature profile across a feedwater heater is shown in Figure 16. Feedwater heaters have two pinch points temperature difference namely, terminal temperature difference and drain cooler. These two pinch points are used as performance indicators for assessment of a feedwater heater.

$$TTD = T_s - T_1 \tag{46}$$

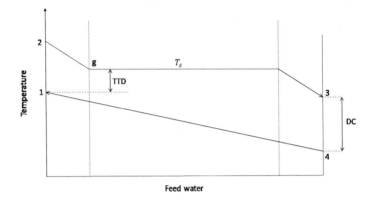

Figure 16. Temperature profile across a feedwater heater .

$$DC = T_3 - T_4 \tag{47}$$

8.4. Deaerator

Two functions are assigned to deaerators in a steam cycle. It works as a feedwater heater as well as removing the oxygen and other dissolved gases from water. Its performance indicators are dissolved gases in the outlet water and its pinch point temperature difference defined as below.

$$TTD = t_s - t_o \tag{48}$$

In which t_o is water outlet temperature and t_s is saturation temperature.

8.5. Gas Air Heater

Gas air heater is a regenerative rotary heat exchanger which is used to preheat air by the flue gas. Due to higher pressure of the air with respect to the gas, air leaks into the flue gas. This leakage increases the flue gas mas flue rate, therefore, decreases the efficiency. The standard supports energy audition of the gas air heaters is ASME PTC 4.3. Leakages may be estimated by measuring flue gas analysis before and after the gas air heater.

$$AL = \frac{lb \ wet \ air \ leakage}{lb \ wet \ gas \ entering \ air \ heater} = \frac{W_{G,l} - W_{G,e}}{W_{G,l}} \tag{49}$$

$W_{G,e}$: Mass of wet gas per mass of fuel entering the air heater

$W_{G,l}$: Mass of wet gas per mass of fuel leaving the air heater

The air leakage reduces flue gas temperature without increasing the efficiency of the HRSG. Gas air heater leaving temperature without leakage may be calculated from equation 50 (ASME, 2007b).

$$T_{gcr} = T_g + \frac{MCP_A}{MCP_{fg}} \left(\frac{M_{fge}}{M_{fgi}} - 1 \right) (T_g - T_{Ai}) \tag{50}$$

T_g: Inlet flue gas temperature to air heater

MCP_A: Mean specific heat of air

MCP_{fg}: Mean specific heat of flue gas

M_{fge}: Outlet mass flow rate of flue gas to the air heater

M_{fgi}: Inlet mass flow rate of flue gas to the air heater

T_{Ai}: Inlet air temperature to the air heater

Comparing the air heater leaving temperature with and without leakage, the efficiency loss regarding the leakages may be estimated practically.

9.   Error Analysis

Energy efficiency of WtE power plant is determined using some parameters in direct and indirect methods. There are some uncertainties in calculated efficiency due to possible errors in measured parameters. The efficiency may be written as a function of measured parameters as presented in equation51.

$$\eta = \eta \left[x_1, x_2, ..., x_n \right] \tag{51}$$

Uncertainty in the procedure of energy efficiency assessment may be estimated as follows (Holman, J. P.):

$$W_\eta = \left[w_1 (\frac{\partial \eta}{\partial x_1})^2 + w_2 (\frac{\partial \eta}{\partial x_2})^2 + ... + w_n (\frac{\partial \eta}{\partial x_n})^2 \right] \tag{52}$$

w_i: Error in the ith estimated parameters

$(\frac{\partial \eta}{\partial x_i})$: Sensitivity of the method to error in estimation of the x_i

10.   Case Study

10.1.   Plant Description

The studied plant consists of two parallel lines, each with capacity of $100\ (ton/day)$ of MSW. As it is shown in Figure 9 ,the MSW is fed into a single step eccentric rotating grate within a compact cylindrical furnace (primary chamber). The MSW drying, pyrolysis, gasification, and combustion processes occurs in this step. Then, The yielded syngas was further burned out in the secondary chamber at around $900 - 1100\ °C$. The resulting flue gas enters an steam generator, producing the steam to run a $3.3\ MW$ steam turbine. Before releasing to the atmosphere, the flue gas passes a 3-stage gas cleaning unit.

10.2.   LHV

The bomb calorimeter used in this study was CAL3K-U. The waste pit were sampled ten times a day, within two weeks and the result can be found in Table 7.

Table 7. Waste sampling normal distribution parameters

Sample count	Min LHV(Btu/lb)	Max LHV(Btu/lb)	Mean value	Confidence level(%)
140	2687.02	3095.44	2894.24	95.0

10.3.   Direct Method

Using the data gathered from the WtE power plant control room (Table 8), the overal efficiency by direct method can be calculated from equation 53.

$$\eta = \frac{3412 \times (TGE - IEC)}{\dot{m}_f LHV_f + \dot{m}_{af} LHV_{af}} = \left(\frac{71627 - 7890}{400000.8 \times 2894.239 + 0.486 \times 40000}\right) = 18.78\%$$
(53)

10.4.   Indirect Method

The efficiency of sub-systems 1 to 3 and the term of internal energy consumption are calculated and finally multiplied by the total system efficiency.

Table 8. Collected data used for the direct method

Symbol	Definition	Unit	Amount
TGE	Total generator electricity production	kWh	71627
IEC	Internal electricity consumption	kWh	7890
M_f	Mass of waste dispose	lb	400000.8
LHV_f	Lower heating value of waste	BTU/lb	2894.239
M_{af}	Mass of auxiliary fuel consumption	lb	0.486
LHV_{af}	Lower heating value of auxiliary fuel	Btu/lb	40000

10.4.1. Steam Generator Audit

The measured data for calculating steam generator efficiency are given in Table 9. Moreover, the computational data required in this method is presented in the table 10. Enthalpy of flue gas and residue were calculated based on data presented in the ASME PTC4.1(ASME, 2008). Additionally, the calculated mean specific heat and enthalpy are given in Table 11 and 12, respectively. The quantity of losses and credits are calculated in Table 13 and 14. The energy loss terms are calculated according to the values reported in Table 15 and the contribution of each term in the overall loss is determined as presented in Figure 17.

$$\eta = 100 - \sum_{i=1}^{11} L_i = 100 - (40.076) = 67.622\% \tag{54}$$

As it is illustrated in Figure 17, the most significant loss terms are related to moisture in waste (L_2) and dry flue gas outlet ($L1$). Then, unburned combustible in residue ($L4$) and sensible heat of residue ($L6$) are on the second level of importance. Finally, the surface radiation and convection ($L7$) and the leachate loss term (L_8) are negligible.

10.4.2. Power Cycle Audit

The main parameters for modeling a steam cycle are pressure and temperature in different points and isentropic efficiencies of the steam turbine and pumps. The required parameters are shown in Table 16 and 17 and 18 and 19.

Table 9. Collected data used for the steam generator

No	Symbol	Description	Unit	Amount
1	$\dot{m}_f$	Mass flow rate of Waste	lb/hr	16666.7
2	$\dot{m}_a$	Mass flow rate of air inlet	lb/hr	78885.2
3	$\dot{m}_r$	Mass flow rate of residue	lb/hr	3306.9
4	$\dot{m}_l$	Mass flow rate of leachate	lb/hr	496.04
5	$\dot{m}_{af}$	Mass flow rate of auxiliary fuel	lb/hr	0.020
6	O_2	Volume percent in flue gas	percent	8.07
7	CO_2	Volume percent in flue gas	percent	14.09
8	CO	Volume percent in flue gas	percent	0.0009
9	T_g	Temperature of flue gas outlet	°F	428
10	T_a	Temperature of air inlet	°F	77
11	T_r	Temperature of residue outlet	°F	887
12	T_{rv}	Temperature of references	°F	77
13	LHV_f	LHV of waste	Btu/lb	2894.24
14	LHV_c	LHV of carbon	Btu/lb	12000
15	LHV_{af}	LHV of auxiliary fuel	Btu/lb	40000
16	m_{wf}	Percentage of moisture in waste	lb/lb	40.5
17	$(H_2O)_l$	Percentage of moisture in leachate	lb/lb	90
18	ω	Absolute humidity	lb/lb	0.015
19	C	Percentage of carbon in waste	lb/lb	23.2
20	C_r	Percentage of carbon in residue	lb/lb	3
21	C_l	Percentage of carbon in leachate	lb/lb	0.5
22	H	Percentage of hydrogen in waste	lb/lb	2.4
23	S	Percentage of sulfur in waste	lb/lb	0.3

Table 10. Calculation data for the steam generator

No	Symbol	Definition	Unit	Calculation	Amount
24	W_{dg}	Flue gas mass per waste mass	lb/lb	$\frac{11[7]+8[6]+7[33]}{3[7]}[28]\frac{12.01[23]}{32.07}$	4.099
25	W_a	Air inlet mass per waste mass	lb/lb	[2]/[1]	4.73
26	W_l	Leachate mass per waste mass	lb/lb	[4]/[1]	0.03
27	W_r	Residue mass per waste mass	lb/lb	[3]/[1]	0.198
28	C_b	Carbon burnt per waste	lb/lb	[19]-([20][27])-([21][26])	0.2257
29	m_{vfg}	Moisture in flue gas per waste	lb/lb	$0.08936[22]+\frac{[16]}{100}-[30]$	0.592
30	m_{wl}	Moisture in leachate per waste	lb /lb	[17] × [26]	0.0243
31	MW_{fg}	molecular weight of flue gas	lb/lbmol	$44.01\frac{[7]}{100}+16\frac{[6]}{100}+28.01\frac{[32]}{100}$	30.573
32	N_2	Percent volume in dry flue gas	percent	100-([6]+[7])	77.84

Turbine Energy Auditing

The steam turbine is a 3.3 MW with maximum working pressure of 580 psia. The required thermodynamic properties from the turbine is collected in Table 16.

Table 11. Mean specific heat for the steam generator

No	Symbol	Definition	Unit	Calculation	Amount
33	MCP_{fg}	Mean specific heat of dry gas leaving	Btu/lbm.F	ASME PTC4.1 enthalpy table	0.2415
35	MCP_r	Mean specific heat of residue	Btu/lbm.F	ASME PTC4.1 enthalpy table	0.2385

Table 12. Enthalpy calculation for the steam generator

No	Symbol	Entalpy	Unit	Calculation	Amount
36	H_{fg}	dry gas leaving	Btu/lb	[33] × ([9] − [12])	84.766
37	H_v	water vapor at 1 psia and Tg	Btu/lb	Steam table	1254.8
38	H_{rv}	water at reference temperature	Btu/lb	Steam table	45
39	H_{va}	water vapor at Tg	Btu/lb	Steam table	159.705
40	H_r	residue	Btu/lb	[35] × ([11] − [12])	193.185

Table 13. Energy losses for the steam generator

Symbol	Energy losses	Unit	Calculation	Amount
Q_1	Dry gas	Btu/lb	[24] × [36]	347.364
Q_2	Moisture in waste	Btu/lb	[29] × ([37] − [38])	713.778
Q_3	Moisture in air	Btu/lb	[18] × [25] × [39]	11.339
Q_4	Unburned combustibles	Btu/lb	[27] × [20] × [14]	71.429
Q_5	Incomplete combustion	Btu/lb	$27.01 \times 4336.89 \times \frac{[8][24]}{31}$	14.695
Q_6	Sensible heat of residue	Btu/lb	[27] × [40]	38.331
Q_7	Radiation and convection	Btu/lb	ASME PTC4.1 figure	0.370
Q_8	Leachate	Btu/lb	[21] × [26] × [14]	1.786
Q_9	Additional moisture	Btu/lb	-	0
Q_{10}	Steam coil air heater	Btu/lb	-	0
Q_{11}	Cooling water	Btu/lb	-	0

Isentropic efficiency of the turbine is calculated as follows.

$$\eta_s = \frac{h_{in} - h_{out}}{h_{in} - h_{out,s}} = \frac{1418.745 - 1107.911}{1418.745 - 1076.526} = 90.83\% \tag{55}$$

Table 14. Credits for the steam generator

Symbol	Credit	Unit	Calculation	Amount
B_1	Dry air	Btu/lb	-	0
B_2	Moisture in entering air	Btu/lb	-	0
B_3	Auxiliary fuel	Btu/lb	$\frac{[5]}{[1]} \times [15]$	809.214

Table 15. Energy loss terms for the steam generator

Symbol	Definition	Amount(%)
L_1	Energy loss term due to dry gas	10.802
L_2	Energy loss term due to moisture in waste	19.273
L_3	Energy loss term due to moisture in air	0.306
L_4	Energy loss term due unburned combustibles in residue	1.929
L_5	Energy loss term due to incomplete combustion	0.397
L_6	Energy loss term due to sensible heat of residue	1.035
L_7	Energy loss term due to surface radiation and convection	0.010
L_8	Energy loss term due to leachate	0.048
L_9	Energy loss term due to additional moisture	0
L_{10}	Energy loss term due to steam coil air heater	0
L_{11}	Energy loss term from cooling water	0

Boiler Feed Pump Energy Auditing

Required parameters for audition of condensor pump are peresented in Table 18.

$$(h_d - h_s) = \frac{\triangle P}{\rho g} = 195073.645 \tag{56}$$

$$P_h = Q(h_d - h_s)\rho g = 41.725 \tag{57}$$

$$\eta_{pump} = \frac{P_h}{P_T} = \frac{41.725}{48.17} = 86.62\% \tag{58}$$

Condenser Pump Energy Auditing

Required parameters for audition of boiler feed pump are peresented in Table 19.

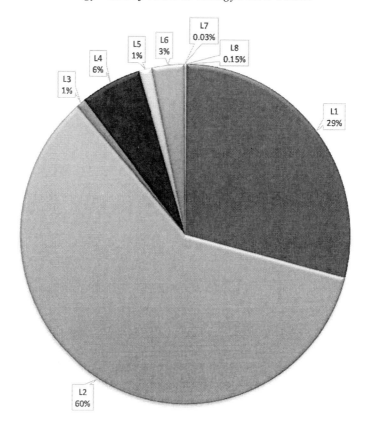

Figure 17. Loss terms for the steam generator.

$$\left(h_d - h_s\right) = \frac{\triangle P}{\rho g} = 11706.0768 \tag{59}$$

$$P_h = Q(h_d - h_s)\rho g = 2.255 \tag{60}$$

$$\eta_{pump} = \frac{P_h}{P_T} = \frac{2.255}{2.65} = 85.09\% \tag{61}$$

Efficiency of Power Cycle

$$\eta = \eta_{cycle} = 32.39\% \tag{62}$$

Table 16. Collected data used for the power cycle

Point no	Quantity	unit	Amount
1	T	$°F$	180
	P	psia	7.67
2	T	$°F$	181
	P	psia	27.5
3	T	$°F$	245
	P	psia	27.5
4	T	$°F$	246
	P	psia	362.6
5	T	$°F$	781.34
	P	psia	291.671
6	T	$°F$	331.4
	P	psia	27.5
7	T	$°F$	180
	P	psia	7.67

Table 17. Collected data used for the steam turbine

Symbol	Definition	Unit	Amount
h_{in}	Enhalpy of steam entering the turbine	Btu/lb	1418.745
h_{out}	Enhalpy of steam exciting the turbine	Btu/lb	1107.911
$h_{out,s}$	Enhalpy of steam isentropic process at the turbine excite	Btu/lb	1076.526

10.4.3.   Electric Generator

Parameters for audition of the electric generator are presented in Table 20.

$$\dot{P}_{out} = TGE - IEC = 71627 - 7890 = 63737 \tag{63}$$

$$\dot{W}_{shaft} = \dot{P}_{out} + Q_{gen} = 63737 + 1911.9 = 65648.9 \tag{64}$$

Table 18. Collected data used for the boiler feed pump energy audit

Symbol	Definition	Unit	Amount
p_{in}	Inlet flow pressure to pump	psia	25.557
p_{out}	Outlet flow pressure of pump	psia	362.594
ρ	Density of flow	lbm/ft^3	59
Q	Volume flow rate of pump	ft^3/sec	0.1238
P_T	Power input to the pump	Btu/sec	48.17

Table 19. Collected data used for the condenser pump energy audit

Symbol	Definition	Unit	Amount
P_{in}	Inlet flow pressure to pump	psia	7.687
P_{out}	Outlet flow pressure of pump	psia	27.557
ρ	Density of flow	lbm/ft^3	60
Q	Volume flow rate of pump	ft^3/sec	0.1134
P_T	Power input to the pump	Btu/sec	2.65

Table 20. Collected data used for the electric generator auditing

Symbol	Definition	Unit	Amount
TGE	Total generator electricity production	kWh	71627
IEC	Internal electricity consumption	kWh	7890
Q_{gen}	Mechanical and electrical losses	kWh	1911.9

Consequently, the efficiency of the generator (η_{gen}) is illustrated as below:

$$\eta_{gen} = 1 - \left(\frac{Q_{gen}}{\dot{W}_{shaft}}\right) = 1 - \left(\frac{1911.9}{65648.9}\right) = 97.09\% \tag{65}$$

10.4.4. Internal Electricity Consumption

Total generator electricity production and internal electricity consumption including fans, cycle pumps, condenser vacuum pump are presented in Table 21

$$\left(1 - \frac{IEC}{TGE}\right) = \left(1 - \frac{7890}{71627}\right) = 88.98\% \tag{66}$$

Table 21. Collected data used for the internal consumption

Symbol	Definition	Unit	Amount
TGE	Total generator electricity production	kWh	71627
IEC	Internal electricity consumption	kWh	7890

10.4.5. Overall System Efficiency

Results of the efficiency calculation and internal electricity consumption are summarized in Table 22.

Table 22. Efficiency of sub-systems

Symbol	Definition	Amount(%)
η_1	Efficiency of steam generator	67.622
η_2	Efficiency of power cycle	32.39
η_3	Efficiency of electric generator	97.08
$1 - \frac{IEC}{TGE}$	Internal electricity consumption	88.98

Finally, the overall power plant efficiency is obtained from equation below.

$$\eta_o = \eta_1.\eta_2.\eta_3 \left(1 - \frac{IEC}{TGE}\right) = 18.92\% \tag{67}$$

Comparing results of the overall efficiency evaluation by direct and indirect methods; it can be observed that efficiency values differ by 0.14 %. This is mainly due to the measurement errors in large-scale WtE power plants in which waste mass flow rate is quite difficult to define accurately, therefore, the results will differ significantly.

Energy diagram of the power plant is presented in Figure 18. It is seen that the biggest sources of the energy loss are heat rejected in the condenser, stack loss due to moisture and heat loss of dry flue gas respectively. Because of low efficiency of the power cycle, the heat rejection in the condenser is rather high. Additionally, the stack loss due to moisture in the fuel may be reduced by using drying process for the waste.

10.5. Error Analysis

In Figure 19 sensitivity of the direct and indirect method to error in waste mass flow as shown.

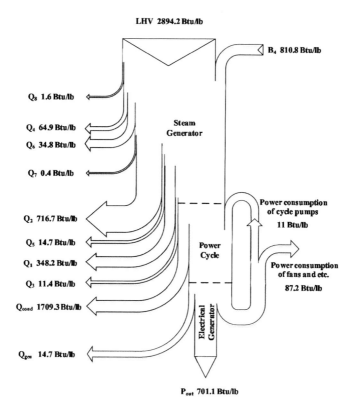

Figure 18. Energy diagram of the studied WtE power plant.

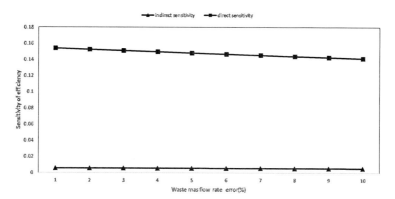

Figure 19. Sensitivity of overall efficiency to waste mass flow rate error.

As it may be seen from the Figure 19, in the indirect method, sensitivity of the efficiency to the measurement error of mass flow rate is significantly lower than that of in the direct method. This means that unlike the direct method, efficiency of the power plant may be estimated more accurately by indirect method despite inaccurate measurement of the waste mass flow rate.

Conclusion

A comprehensive method was presented for energy audition of WtE power plants. The efficiency value in the proposed method was almost insensitive to waste mass flow rate measurement error; therefore, this method is accurate enough for energy audition on a large-scale. The method was applied to a medium size, 200 ton/day, WtE power plant. Efficiency were evaluated by the direct and indirect methods. The value of two efficiencies obtained by the methods were close mainly due to accurate estimation of the waste mass flow rate and a long testing time. However, accurate measurement of the waste mass flow rate may not be practical in large scale WtE power plant. The loss method applied to the steam generator was different with the method suggested by ASME PTC 34. Authors experience in audition of power plants shows that there are normally some limitation in metering equipment of power plants and a single method may not be applicable to all plants. Therefore, the presented method may be advantageous in some audition projects.

References

ASME (1964). *ASME PTC 4.1-b-1964: Fire Steam Generator Performance Test Codes.* American Society of Mechanical Engineers.

ASME (1976). *ANSI/ASME PTC 24-1976 (R1982): Ejectors.* American Society of Mechanical Engineers.

ASME (1978). *ASME PTC 33-1978: Large Incinerators Performance Test Codes.* American Society of Mechanical Engineers.

ASME (1981). *ANSI/ASME PTC 4.4-1981: Gas Turbine Heat Recovery Steam Generator Performance Test Codes.* American Society of Mechanical Engineers.

ASME (1984). *ANSI/ASME PTC 11-1984 (R1995): Fan.* American Society of Mechanical Engineers.

ASME (1990). *ASME PTC 8.2-1990: Centrifugal pumps.* American Society of Mechanical Engineers.

ASME (1996). *ASME PTC 6-1996: Steam Generating Units.* American Society of Mechanical Engineers.

ASME (1997). *ASME PTC 12.3-1997: Performance Test Codes on Dearators.* American Society of Mechanical Engineers.

ASME (2000). *ANSI/ASME PTC 12.1-2000 (R2005): Closed Feedwater Heaters.* American Society of Mechanical Engineers.

ASME (2007a). *ASME PTC 30.1-2007: Air-Cooled Steam Condensers.* American Society of Mechanical Engineers.

ASME (2007b). *ASME PTC 34-2007: Waste Combustors With Energy Recovery Performance Test Codes.* American Society of Mechanical Engineers.

ASME (2008). *ASME PTC 4.1-2008: Fire Steam Generator Performance Test Codes.* American Society of Mechanical Engineers.

ASME (2010). *ASME PTC 12.2-2010: Steam Surface Condensor Performance Test Codes.* American Society of Mechanical Engineers.

Ciuta, S., Tsiamis, D., and Castaldi, M. J. (2017). *Gasification of Waste Materials: Technologies for Generating Energy, Gas, and Chemicals from Municipal Solid Waste, Biomass, Nonrecycled Plastics, Sludges, and Wet Solid Wastes.* Academic Press.

Company, B. W. (1913). *Steam, its generation and use.* Babcock & Wilcox.

Holman, J. P. (1966). *Experimental Methods for Engineers.* New York : McGraw-Hill.

Luque, R. and Speight, J. (2014). *Gasification for Synthetic Fuel Production: Fundamentals, Processes and Applications.* Elsevier.

Rada, E. C. (2017). *Thermochemical Waste Treatment: Combustion, Gasification, and Other Methodologies.* CRC Press.

Reddy, P. J. (2016). *Energy Recovery from Municipal Solid Waste by Thermal Conversion Technologies.* CRC Press.

Sewa Bhawan, R. K. P. (2010). *Energy Performance Assessment For Equipment And Utility Systems.* National Certification Examination For Energy Managers And Energy Auditors.

Speight, J. G. (2014). *Gasification of unconventional feedstocks.* Gulf Professional Publishing.

In: Auditing: An Overview   ISBN: 978-1-53615-116-9
Editors: T. Cavenagh and J. Rymill © 2019 Nova Science Publishers, Inc.

Chapter 4

AUDITING AS A TOOL FOR CLARIFYING ORGANIZATIONS' LEVEL ON COMPREHENSIVE, RISK-BASED SAFETY AND SECURITY MANAGEMENT

Jyri Rajamäki[*]*, PhD and Soili Martikainen, PhD*
Laurea University of Applied Sciences, Espoo, Finland

ABSTRACT

This chapter shows via case examples that auditing is an extremely suitable method for clarifying the level of the comprehensive, risk-based safety and security management (SSM) of organizations operating in business and in public sector. The aim of the Chapter is to encourage organizations to develop their SSM system towards a comprehensive and risk-based approach and to evaluate the level of SSM system through auditing.

In addition, this chapter introduces three tools developed in Finland that can be applied in SSM audits: 1) The SSM framework drawn up by the Confederation of Finnish Industries in which both safety and security

---

[*] Corresponding Author's Email: jyri.rajamaki@laurea.fi.

aspects have been included. The framework is widely used both in business and in public sector. 2) National auditing tool 'Katakri 2015' which is designed for assessing organization's ability to protect an authority's classified information and 3) 'Tutor' model designed for inspection or auditing of the SSM developed by the Finnish rescue authority.

This chapter is based on the study, in which 76 Finnish educational institutions were audited between 2011 and 2014 by using the Tutor model and the SSM framework drawn up by the Confederation of Finnish industries. Moreover, the risk management process in accordance with the standard ISO 31000:2018 has been utilized. Educational institution in the study refers to elementary schools, high schools, vocational schools, universities and universities of applied sciences. Our experience shows that the safety and security matters are typically discussed and decided in fragmented way or in different contexts without emphasizing the development of comprehensive SSM. Furthermore, the risk management has not been implemented to set strategy, nor to achieve objectives and make decisions in all levels of the organization.

Keywords: audit, comprehensive safety and security management, risk, risk management, safety, security

INTRODUCTION

A safe and secure working environment is an obvious requirement seeking both employees and employers. However, the challenge is to establish a comprehensive, risk based safety and security management (SSM) system in an organization. The need of the management system is emphasized by numerous international standards covering, for example, quality, information security, occupational health and safety as well as business continuity management systems (ISO 9000:2015, ISO/IEC 27001:2013, ISO 45001:2018 and ISO 22301:2012). Moreover, risk management is an essential part of setting strategy, achieving objectives and making decisions in different levels of the organization (ISO 31000:2018). Risk management has a vitally important role in any management system. For example, in practice cybersecurity management is a risk management procedure (Kataikko 2017) as Figure 1 presents.

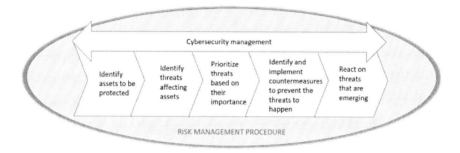

Figure 1. Cybersecurity management as a risk management procedure (adapted from Kataikko 2017).

This Chapter focuses on SSM system to for which there is no international standard available but a management framework made by the Confederation of Finnish Industries. Additionally, in this Chapter it is focused on the 'Katakri 2015' and 'Tutor' audits with which the organizations' level on comprehensive, risk-based SSM can be clarified.

The aim of this Chapter is to encourage organizations to develop their SSM system towards a comprehensive and risk-based approach and to evaluate the level of SSM system through auditing. The object is to present the results of the audit in the Finnish educational institutions targeted to the SSM system.

SAFETY AND SECURITY AUDITING TOOLS

Many different types of audits exist, including financial audits, property assessments, supplier reviews, contractor evaluations, registration audits and equipment evaluations (Russell 2012). Figure 2 illustrates internal (first-party) and external (second-party and third-party) auditing types. The common principle is that they compare applied procedures, as well as a set of collected information, against some established criteria. According to Kohnke, Shoemaker and Sigler (2016) the purpose of the audit is to gather sufficient, reliable, pertinent and practical evidence to demonstrate that defined security and performance control objectives are met.

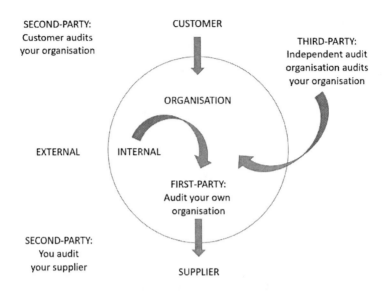

Figure 2. First-second- and third-party audits (adapted from Russell 2012).

Standard ISO/IEC 17021-2:2012 is a normative standard intended for use by accreditation bodies when assessing management systems, while ISO 19011:2018 provides guidelines for first-, second- and third-party auditors when auditing management systems. The third-party certification industry use standard ISO/IEC 17021-1:2015 to define requirements for audits and audit arrangements and, additionally, accreditation bodies will determine whether a certification body's auditing arrangements and activities comply with those requirements. Standard ISO 19011:2018 identifies best practice and provides information on what should be done when carrying out an audit without specifying how it must be done. Continuing development of management systems standards for information security, for example, means that standard ISO 19011:2018 must be able to accommodate differing requirements while still providing useful guidance.

The three things that make a management system audit different from other types of assessments are that the audit must be 1) systematic, 2) independent and 3) documented. In order to conduct systematic management system audits, there is a need for both audit procedures and an audit programme. From an independence point of view, auditors may not audit their own work or that of their colleagues', as there would be a conflict of interest. Audits need to be structured, to ensure they are free from bias and conflicts of interest. Audits must be documented, because they are all about making decisions and taking action (Rajamäki and Rajamäki 2013).

When auditing SSM, different tools can be used as shown in Figure 3.

The first valuable tool for the SSM audit is the SSM framework drawn up by the Confederation of Finnish industries (2016) which resembles various safety and security sections to be taken care of. It also combines SSM, risk management, safety & security culture and business strategy. Another useful tool is Katakri, if the organization has access to confidential information of the authority, for example through projects. Katakri describes the means by which classified information is protected. Instead of Katakri or in addition to it, other applicable standards, such as environmental management standard ISO 14001, occupational health and safety standard ISO 45001 or security management systems standard for the supply chain ISO 28001 may be included in the audit. The third valuable tool for the SSM audit is the Tutor auditing model, which ensures that auditing covers SSM starting from the management commitment through practical measures and continuing to safety & security indicators as well as continuous improvement.

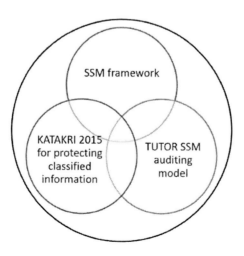

Figure 3. Tools for auditing SSM.

SSM FRAMEWORK

The SSM framework drawn up by the Confederation of Finnish industries (2016) was originally intended for private sector companies, but has been successfully applied to all kind of organizations, both in private and public sector. In Figure 4, in the middle of the circle, the purpose of the framework is mentioned: the objective is to ensure safety and security, continuity and compliance of the organization. The nine sections of the SSM are 1) information security, 2) premises security, 3) compliance control, 4) contingency and crisis management, 5) emergency and preparedness, 6) personnel security, 7) environmental safety, 8) occupational safety and health, as well as 9) security of production and operations. It is emphasized that the safety and security culture is achieved thorough SSM. In the framework, it is underlined that the SSM must be based on the risk management and additionally, on the strategy of the organization. It is also highlighted that SSM is a continuous process following the principles of the PDCA cycle (Confederation of Finnish industries 2016.)

Information security protects the confidentiality, integrity and availability of information of the organization. It may consist of factors such as processing and classification and of information, and evaluation of the significance of various information. Furthermore, information security includes technical information security, administrative information security, data protection and privacy protection, and, furthermore, securing the continuity of operation of systems and processes (Confederation of Finnish industries 2016).

Premises security helps to protect offices and other premises of the organization by using, for example, classification of premises and protecting them by the means of classification, structural security, security surveillance and agreement management. The task of the premises security is to create an undisturbed, secure environment for personnel and visitors, and to prevent theft of information or material, which has value for the organization (Confederation of Finnish industries 2016).

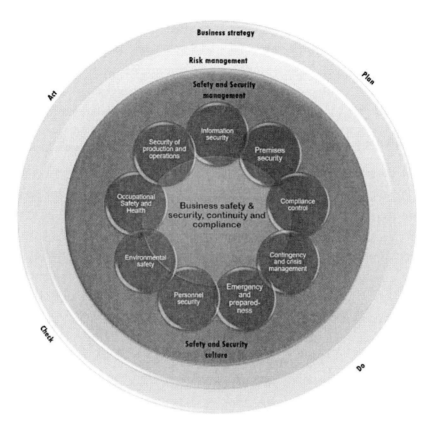

Figure 4. Safety and security management framework (adapted from Confederation of Finnish Industries 2016).

Compliance control protect organization's operation, personnel and property against internal and external threats. It helps the organization to prevent and resolve misuse, crimes and other noncompliant behavior, which have an impact on organization's operation (Confederation of Finnish industries 2016).

Contingency and crisis management is needed by the organization to identify and anticipate unexpected situations and to protect itself by securing the continuity of its operations in all situations. The organization shall sustain its functionality and recover as soon as possible. Business continuity planning, crisis management and contingency planning are important parts of this section (Confederation of Finnish industries 2016).

Emergency and preparedness is needed to prevent fire and other accidents and, moreover, to ensure timely and correct response to accidents. Methods used are, for example, contingency plan, fire protection of buildings, anticipation of potentially dangerous situations, regular training of personnel, creation of safety guidelines, preparedness for major accidents and threat prevention measures. It should be noted that legislation sets some requirements particularly for this section (Confederation of Finnish industries 2016).

Personnel security guarantees safety, security and capability of persons by protecting them from crime and accidents. It also safeguards personnel resources critical to the organization's operation. It may include, for example, protection of employees, customers and key persons from the crime and accidents, safeguarding, as well as securing the continuity of operations by preventing infiltration by criminals (Confederation of Finnish Industries 2016).

Environmental safety covers ecological sustainability, meeting and anticipating environmental expectations of customers and society. These actions are, for example, taking the responsibility for the environment, continuous development of processes, learning from best practices, increasing personnel awareness, committing to the principles of environmental standards and to implement communication with transparency. Environmental safety may consist of waste management, water and soil protection, chemicals control, preventing noise, protecting, landscape climate protection and emissions trading. Additionally, it may include life-cycle thinking, eco balance, and energy efficiency (Confederation of Finnish Industries 2016).

Occupational safety and health includes, among other things, safe work and personnel wellbeing, occupational safety and health organization and, moreover, action programme. Legislation sets some requirements for this section, too (Confederation of Finnish Industries 2016).

Security of production and operations may consist of, for example, product liability and product safety, safety of services as well as security of payment transactions. Furthermore, it may include storage of valuables, transport and storage security, network management, contract management and insurance policies (Confederation of Finnish Industries 2016).

KATAKRI

Katakri is a Finnish information security auditing tool for authorities that is used to determine an organization's ability to protect classified information. It was prepared in cooperation between the Finnish authorities, Finnish industries and specialists in the security field. Katakri has two significant traits that differs from normal standards. Firstly, it makes the actions of responsible authorities work transparent and equal towards everybody. Secondly, it allows Finnish industries to be more cost effective by making the authorities' requirements foreseeable. As Figure 5 shows the requirements in Katakri are divided into three different areas: security management (T), physical security (F) and information assurance (I).

Katakri auditing criteria do not give mandatory requirements on information security, instead it is based on existing Finnish legislation and international information security obligations. Most important of these are – at the national level the Government Decree on Information Security in Central Government (681/2010) which sets the foundation of both national and international Classified Information - and at the international level the Council Decision on the Security Rules for protecting EU Classified Information (2013/488/EU), which lays down principles and minimum standards of security for protecting EU Classified Information (EUCI). It also refers to other commonly known standards such as ISO 27000 -series. The requirements of the information assurance section can be fulfilled according to the three Finnish national protection levels IV, III and II, which are equal to the international levels of classification: RESTRICTED, CONFIDENTAL and SECRET (Katakri 2015).

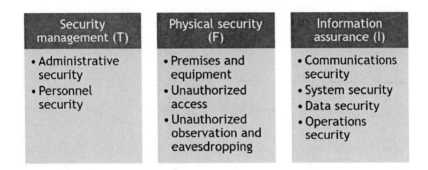

Figure 5. Katakri Information security audit tool.

Katakri can be used as an auditing tool to assess for a Facility Security Clearance (FSC) how an organization's security arrangements are implemented and to assess the authorities' information assurance. It can be used to support and develop companies', organizations' and authorities' security measures, and to ensure that the organization has introduced sufficient security arrangements to prevent unauthorized disclosure of classified information in all the environments where such information is handled. A further goal is to ensure that security requirements are taken into account in security management procedures.

An acceptable security level in view of possible threats can be reached by planning and implementing security arrangements and the organization should demonstrate that in a reliable manner. This shall be based on systematic risk assessment and security risk management shall be used to implement a combination of security measures. This will create a satisfactory balance among user requirements, costs and residual risks. (Katakri 2015). However, experiences indicate that the two-phased risk management process has not been fully utilized as intended and the intended risk management process could have been described more clearly (Kelo & Eronen 2017). In audits performed by the National Communications Security Authority Finland, many organizations seem to emphasize cost-effectiveness in risk management, which increases the responsibilities of the auditing authority (Kelo & Eronen 2017).

TUTOR

The Finnish rescue authority, the Keski-Uusimaa Department for Rescue Services has developed the Tutor model in 2010 with which the SSM system can be inspected by an authority or audited, for example, by an independent third-party auditor. The Tutor model emphasizes that the organization itself has the responsibility for the management of risks, safety and security. Moreover, it is emphasized that preparedness is a key element for maintaining and developing the overall risk-based safety and security (Tutor Max 2011, 2).

A self-assessment is an important part of the Tutor model. The authorities may ask organizations to make a self-assessment prior to their visits or alternatively, as in this study, the organization conducted a self-assessment during the audit with help from the auditor. The management of the audited organization also set objectives for the next three years regarding their safety and security activities. Finally, the auditor gave his /her own evaluation of the performance level of the organization (Tutor Max 2011, 5).

The Tutor model (2012) consists of eight different sections, as follows: 1) SSM, 2) Operational risks, 3) Compliance with requirements, 4) Safety and security documentation, 5) Facility management technology and safety & security technology, 6) Training, 7) Safety and security communication, and 8) Results and effectiveness. In the Tutor model, each section comprises a variable number of topics that are called cards, as they are presented on their own pages.

There are five repeating themes in the Tutor model: risks, stakeholders, reporting, indicators and continuous improvement (Tutor model 2012). In Figure 6, the eight different sections and the five themes of the Tutor model are illustrated.

In the Tutor Max, the largest Tutor model, there are 23 cards in total, in other words, 23 pages divided into eight different sections. There are five cards in section 1, SSM: Planning and control (1.1), management awareness (1.2), monitoring and control of the organization (1.3), resources as well as safety and security organization (1.4) and, finally, cooperation with stakeholders (1.5) (Tutor model 2012).

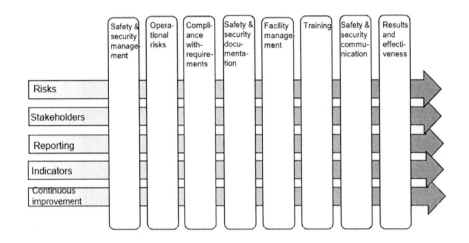

Figure 6. Sections and themes of the Tutor model (Martikainen 2016, 91).

Card 1.1 includes the requirements of the guiding principles for safety and security operations as well as for risk based safety and security planning. Moreover, it consists of the requirements for the role of management control and continuous improvement. Card 1.2 comprises the safety and security reporting procedure and its interval. Card 1.3 includes the requirements for regulatory controls and corrective actions caused by the controls. It also includes requirements for the routine internal controls made by the organization itself and internal and external audits as well as the management's awareness of the current state of safety and security. Card 1.4 covers the adequacy of resources and the designation of responsibilities for safety and security tasks. Card 1.5 includes the requirements to determine whether the organization has identified its safety and security stakeholders and their needs, expectations and responsibilities (Tutor model 2012).

In section 2, Operational risks, in the Tutor Max, there are four cards: objectives and guidelines (2.1), risk management system and comprehensiveness (2.2), risk identification (2.3) and, finally, implementation and effectiveness (2.4). Card 2.1 brings up the objectives of the risk management based on the risk management policy, vision and strategy. Furthermore, the guidelines and instructions set for risk assessment are assessed. Card 2.2 assesses whether the overall risk assessment is made both at the corporate and the unit levels. Card 2.3 investigates the identification of operational risks. The participation of stakeholders is evaluated, too. Moreover, card 2.3 includes the coverage of risk identification, forming a part of enterprise risk management. Card 2.4 comprises the prioritization and categorization of risks, appointing persons in charge, defining schedules and taking the necessary steps to manage risks (Tutor model 2012).

Moreover, in section 3, Compliance with requirements, in the Tutor Max model, there is one card: safety- and security-related regulatory requirements and other relevant guidelines (3.1). It consists of regulatory requirements, their recognition, and the monitoring of changes in legislation (Tutor model 2012).

In section 4 of Tutor Max model, Safety and security documentation, there are two cards: operating models (4.1) and legal documents and plans (4.2). Card 4.1 comprises the requirements for the documentation of the management system, and it identifies the person responsible for the documentation. It also investigates the coverage of safety and security documentation as well as the confidentiality, integrity and availability of safety and security documentation. Card 4.2 includes the requirements for the legal documents that must be available for the members of the organization and its stakeholders. It investigates whether these documents have been put into practice, too. Additionally, it comprises the requirements for the documentation that must form a part of the quality management system and the processes of the management (Tutor model 2012).

In section 5 of Tutor Max model, Facility management technology and safety and security technology, there are four cards: technical systems (5.1), premises for rescue operation (5.2), preparedness (5.3) and outsourced operations (5.4). Card 5.1 covers the appropriateness and operation of the technical systems. It includes the requirements for management's awareness of the need for maintenance and also the implementation of the maintenance. Card 5.2 covers periodic inspections and the requirement of the premises for the rescue operation that must fulfill the requirement of the building permit. Furthermore, it covers the operational ability of the personnel and safety-critical stakeholders. Card 5.3 concerns the organization's ability to protect its personnel in danger. Civil defense shelters, their supplies and the management of shelters are also assessed. In addition, it covers the identification of critical infrastructure. Card 5.4 brings up the need for the management of outsourced services, the responsibilities caused by outsourcing activities and the need for contracts covering safety and security issues (Tutor model 2012).

Furthermore, in Tutor Max model, section 6, Training, there are three cards: planning and organizing of training (6.1), adequacy of the training (6.2) and, lastly, training register and training plan (6.3). Card 6.1 investigates the planning of the safety and security training, and it assesses whether the training is appropriate compared to the risks involved and, additionally, whether the training is planned adequately and comprehensively. Card 6.2 consists of the amount, adequacy and quality of the training. Card 6.3 assesses whether quantitative and qualitative goals have been set for safety and security training and whether they are recorded in the training register (Tutor model 2012).

In section 7 of the Tutor Max model, Safety and security communication, there are two cards: implementation of safety and security communication (7.1) as well as safety and security communication in special situations (7.2). Card 7.1 covers the implementation of safety and security communication as well as its adequacy and comprehensiveness as far as the risks and activities of the organization are concerned. Card 7.2 investigates crisis communication, its adequacy and its implementation (Tutor model 2012).

Finally, in Tutor Max model, section 8, Results and effectiveness, there are two cards: monitoring and measurement (8.1) and analysis and improvement (8.2). Card 8.1 addresses the need of monitoring and measurement of the safety and security activities in the organization. It assesses the existence of a monitoring and measuring system and also agreed responsibilities. Card 8.2 comprises analysis and improvement. It includes the requirement of safety and security indicators that are to be analyzed and used effectively as well as the requirement of continuous improvement (Tutor model 2012).

The organizations to be assessed obtain scores from all cards. The scores vary from 1 to 5, and a half-point interval is used. The arithmetical mean of each section is calculated. Eventually, a total arithmetical mean covering all sections is calculated, and thus the overall performance level of the SSM is determined. There are five different performance levels: Weak (level 1), Incomplete (level 2), Basic (level 3), Committed (level 4), and Forerunner (level 5) in the Tutor model (2012), as shown in Figure 7. The minimum acceptable level is Basic (level 6).

In the first level, Weak, the SSM is at an early stage. The identification of principles, needs and requirements are missing. Furthermore, the responsibilities are not designated as far as safety and security activities are concerned. In the second level, Incomplete, the development of the SSM has been started. Principles, needs and requirements are identified, but they are recorded partly inadequately. Moreover, there is fragmentation in the safety and security activities. In the third level, the minimum acceptable level, Basic, principles, needs and requirements are identified and recorded. Additionally, the responsible persons have been designated. In this level, safety and security form a part of everyday activities, and a reporting system operates on a regular basis. In the fourth level, Committed, safety and security can be seen in everyday activities. Furthermore, safety and security matters are regularly reported and the role of the management is emphasized. Safety and security activities are also constantly developed. At the top, in the fifth level, Forerunner, a true SSM system exists. Safety and security form a part of the organization's integrated management system. Moreover, the organization is a role model for other organizations (Tutor Max 2011; Tutor model 2012).

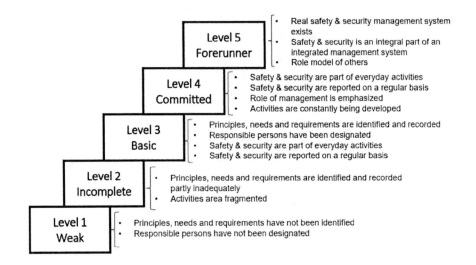

Figure 7. Performance levels of the SSM according to the Tutor model (Martikainen 2016, 96).

EMPIRICAL CASES

In this study, the Tutor model and the SSM framework drawn up by the Confederation of Finnish industries (2016) were used when auditing 76 Finnish educational institutions between 2011 and 2014. These educational institutions were universities of applied sciences (UASs), elementary schools (ESs) as well as high schools, vocational schools and universities which area referred to as other educational institutions. Katakri was not applied in this study, because only universities and universities of applied sciences may have projects in which classified information could be received from authorities.

In Table 1, the overall performance level of the SSM in the audited educational institutions are presented.

The overall performance level of the SSM in the audited educational institutions varied between 1.4 and 3.9, while the minimum acceptable level is 3.0 according to the Tutor model. The overall performance level between was between 1.4 and 3.1 in all except one audited educational institution. Three (3.9%) audited educational institutions out of 76 met the minimum acceptable performance level of 3.0. Only one of these educational institutions, one UAS, reached the overall performance level of 3.9 of the SSM. One UAS received a total score of 3.1, and yet in one section the score was less than 3.0. Additionally, one ES received a total score of 3.1, and yet it had three sections scores of which were less than 3.0. (Martikainen 2016, 129).

Table 1. Overall performance level of SSM in the educational institutions based on auditor's assessment (Martikainen 2016, 129)

Educational institution	N	Minimum score	Maximum score	Mean score (M)	Standard deviation (SD)
Universities of applied sciences	19	1.4	3.9	2.51	0.54
Elementary schools	48	1.6	3.1	2.09	0.29
Other educational institutions	9	1.5	2.6	2.16	0.34

CROSS-CASE ANALYSIS

According to the research findings, there are uniting and separating factors in terms of the SSM between UASs and ESs. For both levels of educational institutions, the most significant developing areas were Training, Results & effectiveness and Operational risks sections. Both levels of educational institutions received moderate scores for the Facility management technology and safety & security technology, SSM and Safety & security communication sections. UASs received the best score in the Compliance with requirements section, while ESs received the best score in the Safety & security documentation section (Martikainen 2016, 129-130).

The audited educational institutions have many development areas in the SSM, and all sections according to the Tutor model required development efforts. As far as the SSM section is concerned, safety and security policy was mostly missing. The SSM was fragmented. Moreover, planning, reporting and control of safety and security activities were minor. There was a lack of internal safety and security checks and inspections. More cooperation with stakeholders was also needed. In addition, the safety and security needs of stakeholders should have been examined. Mainly in the ESs, there was also lack of resources. As far as the Operational risks section is concerned, a risk management system should have been developed. Risk identification was fragmented and mainly based on occupational health and safety as well as fire safety. In the Compliance with requirements section, contact persons for monitoring changes in legislation were not nominated. Moreover, in addition to e-mail, other means for sharing information on changes in legislation were needed. In the Safety and security documentation section, there was a need for the establishment of a documentation management system through which one could recognize a need for valid safety and security documentation. Moreover, documentation was missing on safety and security checks and inspections made by the personnel. There were only a few quick safety and security instructions for substitute teachers. In the Facility management technology and safety & security technology section, challenges arose when the educational institution did not own the facility and neither the facility management nor the janitor were employees of the educational institution. In these cases, the members of the educational institution were not well aware of the status of the maintenance system of the facility. In the Training section, the biggest challenges were the planning and adequacy of the training compared to risks. Moreover, there was a need to establish a training register. Additionally, the task-specific safety and security competence requirements were not identified. In the Safety and security communication section, it was noted that the identification of needs, other than crisis communication needs, were minor. Active, two-way safety and security communication with stakeholders was also one of the development areas. Furthermore, implementation of positive, informative communication was needed, through which a positive safety and security culture could be created. Finally, in the Results and effectiveness section, the most important development areas were the monitoring, measurement and analysis of the comprehensive SSM. (Martikainen 2016, 130-131).

In the audited educational institutions, there were strengths, too. Educational institutions were aware of the importance of the SSM, and the rectors knew that the safety and security of the educational institution were part of their responsibility. Self- evaluation and the setting of future targets in the SSM were realistic. Safety and security handbooks were prepared, and safety and security documentation was plentiful. Risk identification was made with regard to occupational safety and health. Safety drills were held regularly. Additionally, property maintenance system existed. Safety training was held, and fire inspections by the authorities were made regularly (Martikainen 2016, 131).

CONCLUSION

The results of the study shows that SSM is still fragmented in educational institutions in Finland. It is the responsibility of several persons and nobody has an overall picture of its state. Risk management has not been implemented to the processes of the organization to achieve objectives nor make decisions. According to our experience, similar observations have been made in other organizations in Finland after this study. Furthermore, in the study it was found that using auditing tools, such as the SSM framework, Katakri and the Tutor SSM auditing model, help auditor's work to focus on comprehensive, risk-based SSM, its activities and results. Self-assessment of the organization guided by the auditor was found to be a useful task. It taught the auditee to identify development needs itself and thus take the responsibility for the SSM development work.

Various criteria have been developed for designing, implementing and auditing different parts of organizations' SSM. Most of them are based on specific legislation, such as occupational safety and health, fire safety, environmental safety or data protection requirements. Guidance exists how to select relevant criteria. However, from criteria users' point of view, there is a lack of guidance how to apply these criteria simultaneously, - especially when there are conflicting requirements; for example, physical acces control procedures during fire alarm situations in occupational safety and health versus data protection requirements.

Various criteria will be updated on a regular basis, but the development of criteria is inadequately supported by currently available guidance. Kelo, Eronen and Rousku (2018) propose a model for the development of security audit criteria. Their model consists of criteria design goals and concrete implementation guidelines to achieve these goals. This model could be used after modification within other areas of the SSM framework. However, from criteria developers' point of view, another model is needed for developing every SSM related criteria so that they are designed for applying simultaneously having no conflicting requirements.

SSM, business continuity management and risk management systems are based on probabilistic quantitative methods and they are useful for dealing with foreseeable and calculable stress situations. However, they are no longer sufficient to address the evolving nature of risks in the modern cyber-physical world having non-foreseeable and non-calculable stress situations. Also, the high level of interconnectivity in modern society with complexities of large integrated cyber-physical systems (CPS) has opened many avenues for cyber-attacks. Therefore, the issue of cyber-security is currently having, and will continue to have, a major impact on all organizations and the whole organized society. Safety and security thinking has been based on the supposition that we are safe and secure, and we are able to prevent "the bad touch." The focus of actions have been to control one's own systems, to improve protection, and to stay inside this circle of protection. However, nobody alone is able to fully control complex large integrated cyber-physical systems; coordination and cooperation are needed. This means that the focus of the safety and security thinking should be shifted from controlling and securing one's own assets to cooperation and information sharing between the different stakeholders, which is the only way to promote more resilient complex systems of systems. From the above mentioned reasons, we have an urgent need to complement the existing knowledge-base of business continuity and risk management by developing frameworks and models enabling network-wide resilience management. In the future, resilience management should be used to allocate resources to enhance safety, security and resilience, and we need auditing mechanisms for resilience management systems.

REFERENCES

Publications

Confederation of Finnish Industries. 2016. *Safety and security management framework.* Helsinki: Confederation of Finnish Industries.

ISO 9000:2015. *Quality management systems - Fundamentals and vocabulary.* Switzerland: International Organization for Standardization.

ISO 22301:2012. *Societal security. Business continuity management systems. Requirements.* Switzerland: International Organization for Standardization.

ISO/IEC 27001:2013. *Information technology. Security techniques. Information security management systems. Requirements.* Switzerland: International Organization for Standardization.

ISO 31000:2018. *Risk management. Guidelines.* Standardization. Switzerland: International Organization for Standardization.

ISO 45001:2018. *Occupational health and safety management systems - Requirements with guidance for use.* Switzerland: International Organization for Standardization.

Kelo, T., and Eronen, J. 2017. Experiences from Development of Security Audit Criteria, *16th European Conference on Information Warfare and Security*, Academic Conferences and Publishing International Limited, Reading, 208-215.

Kelo, T., Eronen, J., and Rousku, K. 2018. Model for Efficient Development of Security Audit Criteria, *17th European Conference on Information Warfare and Security*, Academic Conferences and Publishing International Limited, Reading, 244-252.

Kohnke, A., Shoemaker, D., and Sigler, K. 2016. *The Complete Guide to Cybersecurity Risks and Controls.* New York: Auerbach Publications.

Rajamäki, J., and Rajamäki, M. 2013. National Security Auditing Criteria, Katakri: Leading Auditor Training and Auditing Process. *12th European Conference on Information Warfare and Security*, Academic Conferences and Publishing International Limited, Reading, 217-223.

Russell, J. P. 2012. *The ASQ auditing handbook.* Fourth Edition. Quality Press.

Tutor Max. 2011. *Pelastusviranomaisen valvontasuunnitelman mukainen turvallisuustoiminnan riskienarviointimalli – Tutor Max (suurasiakasversio). Etukäteen asiakkaalle toimitettava informaatioesite.* Keski-Uudenmaan pelastuslaitos. [*Tutor Max. 2011. Rescue Authority's Control Plan in Accordance with Risk Assessment Model - Tutor Max (Version for Large Customer). Information to be submitted to the customer in advance* (in Finnish).] Vantaa: Keski-Uudenmaan pelastuslaitos. pp. 2-3, 5.

Tutor model. 2012. *Pelastusviranomaisen valvontasuunnitelman mukainen Tutor-arviointi. Max versio.* [*Tutor assessment according to the rescue supervision plan. Max version.* (in Finnish.)] Vantaa: Keski-Uudenmaan pelastuslaitos.

Electronic Media

Kataikko, M. 2017. *Cyber Security in Health Care: From Threat to Opportunity.* Viewed on November 29, 2018 from https://tapahtumat.tekes.fi/uploads/a7d8a1176/Mika_Kataikko-1006.pdf.

Katakri 2015. *Information security audit tool for authorities.* Viewed on November 12, 2018 from https://www.defmin.fi/files/3417/Katakri_ 2015_Information_security_audit_tool_for_authorities_Finland.pdf.

Martikainen, S. 2016. *Development and Effect Analysis of the Asteri Consultative Auditing Process – Safety and Security Management in Educational Institutions.* Dissertation. Acta Universitatis Lappeenrantaensis 691. Lappeenranta: Lappeenranta University of Technology. Viewed on November 12, 2018 from https://lutpub.lut.fi/handle/10024/120710.

INDEX

A

added value, viii, 1, 2, 10, 11, 12, 23, 25, 29, 32
anti-bias training, 60, 62, 64
audit, iii, v, vii, viii, ix, x, 1, 3, 4, 5, 6, 7, 9, 10, 11, 12, 13, 14, 16, 17, 18, 20, 22, 23, 24, 25, 26, 27, 28, 29, 30, 31, 32, 34, 35, 36, 37, 40, 43, 44, 45, 47, 48, 49, 50, 51, 52, 53, 54, 56, 57, 63, 64, 72, 74, 77, 79, 81, 83, 85, 87, 89, 91, 92, 95, 97, 99, 101, 102, 103, 105, 107, 108, 109, 110, 113, 114, 115, 116, 117, 119, 121, 123, 125, 126, 127, 128, 129, 133, 134, 135, 140, 143, 144, 145, 146, 147
audition, vii, ix, 77, 78, 79, 80, 90, 91, 102, 103, 104, 107, 108, 116, 118, 122

B

bias audit, 61

C

change agent, 18, 26, 29
Chief Audit Executive (CAE), 9, 27, 45, 56

cognitive bias, v, vii, ix, 18, 37, 38, 39, 40, 41, 42, 43, 44, 45, 48, 52, 54, 56, 57, 58, 63, 64, 69
cognitive bias codex, 40, 54, 69
comprehensive safety and security management, 126
continuous auditing, 2, 10, 16, 28
control problem of management, 14
credit, 43, 99, 100, 116

D

debiasing, 38, 40, 42, 58, 59, 60, 61, 63, 70, 73, 74
dual compliance, 17
duplication of controls, 24

E

effectiveness, 2, 5, 14, 22, 23, 25, 35, 43, 44, 45, 51, 70, 134, 135, 136, 138, 141, 143
electric generator, ix, 88, 90, 104, 105, 118, 119, 120
energy loss, viii, ix, 77, 78, 80, 89, 91, 94, 95, 96, 97, 98, 113, 120

THE RISE OF ACCOUNTING, AUDITING, AND FINANCE: KEY ISSUES AND EVENTS THAT SHAPED THESE PROFESSIONS FOR OVER 200 YEARS SINCE 1800

AUTHOR: Lal Balkaran

SERIES: Business, Technology and Finance

BOOK DESCRIPTION: With over 200 professional associations, 120 pieces of authoritative literature, 65 well-known fraud cases, 62 accounting firms (including the origins and growth of the "Big Four"), 55 regulatory statutes, 30 frameworks, and much more, this unique book shows in a chronological sequence a range of select issues and events that have impacted and led to the growth of the professions of accounting, auditing, and finance since 1800.

HARDCOVER ISBN: 978-1-53614-732-2
RETAIL PRICE: $160

RESTRUCTURING COMPANIES: METHODS OF IMPROVING EFFICIENCY

AUTHOR: Zbigniew Kuryłek, Ph.D.

SERIES: Business, Technology and Finance

BOOK DESCRIPTION: This monograph raises issues concerning definitions and types of enterprises' efficiency as well as their restructuring processes. It focuses on restructuring and how that process should be carried out in a company to be satisfactory.

SOFTCOVER ISBN: 978-1-53613-811-5
RETAIL PRICE: $95

Asset Management: Strategies, Opportunities and Challenges

EDITOR: Maria Cristina Arcuri

SERIES: Business, Technology and Finance

BOOK DESCRIPTION: This book aims to provide an overview of asset management by focusing on some of the main issues in the sector. It gathers contributions on the system, strategies, opportunities and challenges.

HARDCOVER ISBN: 978-1-53614-246-4
RETAIL PRICE: $160

Financial Crises and Programs: Developments, Analyses and Research

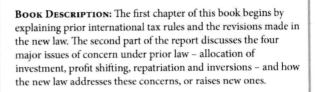

AUTHOR: Patricia Hall

SERIES: Business, Technology and Finance

BOOK DESCRIPTION: The first chapter of this book begins by explaining prior international tax rules and the revisions made in the new law. The second part of the report discusses the four major issues of concern under prior law – allocation of investment, profit shifting, repatriation and inversions – and how the new law addresses these concerns, or raises new ones.

HARDCOVER ISBN: 978-1-53614-159-7
RETAIL PRICE: $160